THE SECRET OF HAPPINESS

DR. YADUVIR SINGH

The book, "The Secret of Happiness", is dedicated to the God, and to the entire humanity.

Contents

Foreword — *vii*

Preface — *xi*

Acknowledgements — *xiii*

Prologue — *xv*

1. The Process Of Life — 1

2. Anxieties And Worries — 5

3. Sufferings — 8

4. Problems And Solutions — 11

5. Success And Failure — 14

6. Faith, Hope And Courage — 17

7. Growth And Excellence — 21

8. Be The Original — 23

9. Good Spouse — 27

10. A Good Family — 30

11. Good Deeds — 33

12. A Good Life — 36

13. Earthly Life And The Afterlife — 40

14. Freewill And The Choices — 43

15. Eternity — 46

16. Well-being — 49

17. Divinity — 51

18. Smile — 53

19. Love — 56

20. Hope — 59

Contents

21. Silence   62

22. Health   65

23. Positivity   69

24. Good Habits   73

25. Habit Of Giving   76

26. Sharing Is Caring   78

27. Killing The Anger   80

28. Turning Weakness Into Strength   83

29. Good Relationships   86

30. Happiness   89

31. Change   92

32. Mind   96

33. Time   99

34. Space   102

35. Age   105

36. Let The Existence Do Not Become Accidental   108

37. I Am The Divine Flame   111

38. The Farewell   114

39. Refuel Your Soul   117

40. Hard Work   119

41. Learn To Live Alone   122

42. Be Creative   126

43. The Secret Of Happiness   129

44. Amazing Life Secrets   134

Foreword

The book, "The Secret of Happiness" gives a clear and effective explanation of the life and happiness. The book, "The Secret of Happiness" is first book of its kind, which discusses all practical aspects related to the Growth and Excellence, Good Life, Success and Failure, Good Deeds, Love, Hope, Amazing Secrets of Life etc.. Spirits, death, life, happiness and karma always had been very interesting topics full of many secrets, and less understood by the majority of beings. Life, Karma and the Happiness are the essence of spirituality. Karma is the basis of whole creation. Thinking creates action(s). Thinking and action create Karma. The reader will get to know some amazing facts related to the happiness and the life after reading this book, "The Secret of Happiness". The author has nicely sequenced and described the topics chapter wise. Divinity, Silence and the Good Habits have been clearly explained. Time and Space have been described in a very clear and effective manner. People in general are ignorant of the design and secrets of the creation. Secret of Happiness is one of the biggest secrets of the life. All enlightened beings live their lives same way. Yoga and meditation are the best ways to lead a contented and joyful life. Meditation acts as a very precise better quality data filter, and thus, making a being, more mindful and happier than before. Death is actually not a loss. Beings always live in one's memory, subconscious and the unconscious mind. One can always reach to a dead loved one, through his or her subconscious mind. Inner talk establishes the communication with the dead being. Memories never die. Love never dies. Pain felt, is due to the love, but in the state of true love, i.e. the unconditional love, there should be no pain. Be thankful to the God, the nature, the existence for bringing that being in the life. Every being comes with his or her fixed journey of the life. Birth brings the death, and then, death brings the next birth, i.e. the rebirth, and thus, the drama of the life and the existence, goes on. Everything, every process is cyclical in the nature, and not linear.

This book, "The Secret of Happiness" makes very lucid discussions about various scientific and spiritual aspects related to the life, relationships and the health. People working in the areas of psychology, cognition, neuroscience, religion and spiritualism will find this book as a ready reckoner and a guide, and an important handbook. Definitely this book is a very rich addition in the intellectual closet of all the reader. This book is meant for entire humanity. In near future, some more good books on other life important and humanity related topics are expected from the author. The author, every other time, raises his own bar and the threshold, by creating another masterpiece, much to his name and credit. Spiritual beings do not run after success and glory, as it comes to them automatically due to their thoughts and actions. They are under constant divine guidance and blessings, and are being decreed by the God, to do the needed things in their given life.

The day, science will be able to explain the beings, about birth, life and the death, to their best levels of understanding and satisfaction, science will replace their religions, and then, the science itself will become their one undisputable religion.

Definitely, the readers will find it a very interesting book on this rare topic of The Secret of Happiness, with many takeaways for their implementation in their daily lives. This book, "The Secret of Happiness" is a treasure trove, a precious gift by the author to the entire humanity.

- Baba

22 / 03 / 2022

Preface

This book, "The Secret of Happiness" is a comprehensive discussion about the process of life, anxieties and worries, sufferings, problems and solutions, success and failures, faith hope and courage, growth and excellence, good spouse, good life, good deeds, divinity, smile, love, hope silence, health, positivity, good habits, silence, time, space, age and the secrets of happiness. World of a being is the set of his or her life experiences. No two beings have similar experiences and learning, or similar life. Beings come into the existence to live by themselves, and to support others to live meaningfully. Life creates experiences, and these experiences must bring happiness. Happiness is the goal and the very purpose of the life. Physical possessions, wealth, worldly relations and attachments can never bring the happiness in the life, but one's religious and spiritual accomplishments bring the satisfaction and the happiness. Live the life with full understanding. Spirituality is quite essential in the life, in order to explore the life, love the life, and live the life meaningfully. Happiness is never external, but purely internal. Overthinking steals the happiness. Do not create the walls, but live in openness, i.e. in the state of complete freedom. God has provided every single thing in the life to enjoy and to share, and not for amassing and storage. More conclusions we make, less alive we become. If something is doable, then do it with full involvement. It would be very remiss of beings, if they do not perform their duties sincerely with complete awakening, and in the state of full consciousness. Life is a game, understand it like a game only, and play it well. Mind is not a dustbin. Do not keep jealousy, hatred or anger into it. Mind is a treasure box. Keep sweet memories, happiness and unconditional love into it. Spending time on hobbies improves one's mental health, and also, the overall well-being. Practise various methods of spirituality and empower the self.

This book, "The Secret of Happiness" is a great gift from the author to the entire humanity in today's times, when there is fierce professionalism, immense competition, tremendous fear, overwhelming stress, deepest levels of anxiety, weakest and most fragile bonds of relationships, heightened levels of distrust, hatred and lowest levels of mutual respect, high ego, no self-esteem and dignity, no integrity in actions, biases and prejudices, unethical practices and hypocrisy at their peak, and cynicism getting reflected all over in the human thought process.

This book, "The Secret of Happiness" is a best pick of its times from the bookstores, and a must read for all. I wish all the readers, a happy reading experience while going through every word, line, paragraph and chapter of the book, "The Secret of Happiness". Reader will feel happy and empowered while reading this book. Power is always of the soul. It is the power of the mind, which runs the whole show of life. Reader will not be able to stop, reading it again and repeating many chapters. Read and explain the book to the members of family, relatives and friends, and gift "The Secret of Happiness" to them, and also, to the others.

- **Dr. Yaduvir Singh**

25 / 02 / 2022

Acknowledgements

The contents of this book, "The Secret of Happiness" are the results of learning and understanding and experiences about the happy life of the author. However, one may always differ from that, what is written. Also, author tenders his sincere apologies in anticipation, if any content is contrary to their faith, belief, knowledge, information, experiences, and hurts their sentiment in any manner. The author will like to acknowledge, all visible and invisible forces, and powers of this existence for providing information, experiences, encouragement and support. The author will like to acknowledge all sources of information, inspiration, which gradually developed author's understanding over many years, along with the experiences. The author also disclaims the responsibility for any loss or damage or harm, if any. Last but not the least, and also, much above everything and all, nothing is possible without the God's will. Author with full servility, respect, gratitude and surrender to the God, puts this book, "The Secret of Happiness" on the holy feet of the God. All is of the God only.

Prologue

This book, "The Secret of Happiness", is a gem in itself, a marvellous intellectual creation par excellence, and a must read book for all, and also, a worthy collection. It is a rare book on a very interesting topics like the process of life, anxieties and worries, sufferings, problems and solutions, success and failures, health, positivity, good habits, silence, time, space, age and the secrets of happiness. This life, nature, universe and the entire creation are too intriguing and mysterious. This book, "The Secret of Happiness" discusses faith hope and courage, growth and excellence, good spouse, good life, good deeds, divinity, smile, love, hope silence and many other important and relevant topics related to the life and the design of the existence. A reading of this book, "The Secret of Happiness" will develop the reader's proper understanding about the real me, life and relationships, karma and death, and happiness. The book, "The Secret of Happiness" has given simple explanations of various aspects related to the mind, thinking, God and the journey of life. The reader will find the book too involving, informative, and also, recreational. Books are the best friends of human beings. Book makes a reader travel through all its contents, and experience the whole journey of reading by him or herself even without lifting the feet. Loosen up, and lose yourself in the book, "The Secret of Happiness", find yourself there, and get benefitted in the life. Keep learning and stay happy in the life.

CHAPTER ONE

The Process Of Life

Life is, what happens to it, when you are too busy making other plans. In the middle of all, unexpectedly, something very bad happens. It is the design of life. In life, there is nothing to get happy, or to get sad. Just witness the life the way it is. We all are passengers in the journey of life, and get down, at the destinations, not consciously known to us, but well known to the nature and the universe. Nature knows everything. Creation cannot happen from nothingness, but needs something, therefore, creation entails destruction. Death is needed for rebirth. Things are cyclical in this existence; however, in every stage of the life i.e. a new creation, there are some differences in what is being created from its immediate past created form. Also, it is not logical to repeat the same created form again. In the game of life, when someone loses, other being wins. Similarly, when one dies, someone is born. As victory is another form of defeat, similarly, birth is another form of the death. No being's life has set patterns of the life. Life is a rollercoaster ride, sometimes up, other times down, never known before, when. It happens with every being without exception. It happened with all great souls and the incarnations of the god, which descended on the earth. All the lessons of the life can be learnt from the nature.

Make the God, your partner, for everything in the life. Choices play a very important role in the game of life. One can choose to be happy, or can even choose to remain sad. Shift the attention, from something which is bad, to something which is good, in order to become cheerful. We create our own lives. Life has no set definitions. Life has no set goals either. Life is a kaleidoscope, with the changing patterns, its changing designs, therefore changing physical goals. What is material or physical will change, and what is non-material or spiritual is permanent. Peace, happiness, joy, satisfaction, love are non-material. Success and failure are material, or physical. In essence, we are spiritual beings in our physical garbs. Our core or the essence never dies. Only what is physical, dies. We are the creation of the planet. What we are, everything has been taken from the planet and the universe. We and the nature are not distinct, but one and the same. Therefore, what is gathered from the planet has to be returned to the planet bit by bit and the time of death. Live the life, the way the nature works, and there will be no problems in the life. Be in sync with the nature and its processes. Have a sense of acceptance, and the gratitude, as doing these, simply brings peace, joy and the happiness in the life. We are one-time born spirits. This spirit has to pass through infinite times and spaces, before it merges back with its source, and then, we are not born again. There is a physical world, where we all live, i.e. earth, and it is a lower dimension. There are certain higher dimensions too, viz. the world of creation, the world of enlightenment, and the spirit world. These three worlds have their rulers, i.e. a ruler spirit. It is the concept of trio. When the God listens to our prayers, he gives us, what is wished for, but when the God does not listen to our prayers, he gives us something even much better.

Therefore, do not settle for less. And when, the God says wait to our prayers, he gives the best. Life is all about its management, i.e. no regrets, no worries, only lessons and the experiences, just acceptance, no expectations and just gratitude; the journey of life is too short. Content of the life does not change the life, rather, context of the life changes the life, therefore, add or create the context of the life which brings joy, peace and the happiness. Work on the inner, as it is the inner, which is every time experienced outside. The things happening outside should not affect the inside, but the inner must influence what is outside the body. Life becomes, as is created. Intelligence and the capability are of no meaning in the life, if one does not have the motivation, courage and the commitment, good enough to convert the possibilities into the reality. Life has to be explored and consciously created, and it is not served readymade on a platter. Life is a struggle. No beings life has ever been simple. Hardships are the part of life. Do not become outcome-oriented, but become input-oriented. Inputs create the output or the outcomes. Output does not create the inputs. Remaining outcome-oriented may be too frustrating, upsetting, discouraging and demotivating at times, whereas remaining input-oriented is too gratifying. Work on the process. Outcome gets automatically created, based on, what the input is. Life is an outcome of our efforts, i.e. thoughts and actions, i.e. the karma. There is always a certain processing time, small or big, for creating the output(s), once the inputs have gone into the process. That is why, unpaid or unsettled karma of a given lifetime, travel to later lifetimes for settlement. The process of life is continuous, as the life itself is continuous. It goes up to infinity. Life is eternal. Because, I always exist, so does this cosmos, today, always and infinitely. For the enlightened beings, the process of life is too simple to comprehend, but for the normal beings, the process of life is too baffling. Therefore, just do, what comes your way, in the best possible ways, with honesty, integrity, humility, morality and the gratitude, and the happiness will automatically follow. Happiness is not the cause, but the effect, i.e. result of thoughts, choices and the actions.

CHAPTER TWO

Anxieties And Worries

Do not hurry, and do not worry. The time will come, when the things will start taking the shape, as wished for. However, keep putting constant efforts. Everything happens at its time, and at the right time, in the journey of the life. Everything that happens, is for good. All big events are planned by the God, and for our best, in the process of life. We are an insignificant element of the creation, yet, creation exists because we exist. All the major events of the life, like birth, death, serious diseases etc., are based on certain divine calculations, which use cosmic intelligence. Never ever we are too early, and also, too late, for anything. It is a continuously changing creation, and nothing is fixed here. Change is the only constant in this existence. Everything is uncertain here. This existence is a play of energies. We are also energies. Always generate and send good and positive energies. Anxieties and worries create a negative energy. It weaken the aura of the being, as a result, such a being can easily become prey to the negative evil forces and energies. He or she will get sick after some time, and may even succumb to death. Understand the phenomenon of life. Anxieties and worries suck on the life, till the life finishes. If something can be done, why to worry, and if, it cannot be done, then also, why to worry.

Beings have developed the habit of worrying for the worries. Anxieties and worries are the enemies of the happiness, and also, of the life. Anxieties and worries are the negative creations of the mind. Do not get trapped in these. Manage the mind. Do not take the life seriously, but only take it sincerely. Negative and negativity are the creations of the mind. Manage the mind in order to perceive everything as positive, and with positivity. Positive thinking is very powerful. Control the stresses. Drink lots of water. Eat fresh fruits. Eat less. Do lots of physical work. Play sports. Do Yoga and meditation. Pray to the God. Talk to the nature, see and observe the things around, and get enchantingly enamoured. Take a walk in the forest. Do morning and evening works. Try to live alone also. Loneliness has great benefits too. One can only reach his or her equilibrium in the loneliness. In togetherness, our real me or I, is lost. Do not avoid others, but at the same time, carve out some time for the self, i.e., I, me and myself, and for the nature. Be comfortable with others. Life's purpose is to teach the unlearnt lessons. Be good to all. Do not hurt anybody. What we give, only returns to us. Learn to control the emotions. Mind has memory. Mind creates the imaginations. Let the memories and the imaginations do not ruin the life. There is no need to worry about the past and the future. Past cannot be undone, and the quality of the future, depends on the quality of present. Control the thoughts and the emotions. Let these do not dominate the life. Realise the nature of the life. Try to know the things in their entirety, and do not have too many physical things, for lasting happiness in the life. Involvement creates happiness. Pay attention to the things of the nature. Try establishing sync with all these, as it then helps in creating the sync among the being's body, mind and the spirit. We as the beings are definitely not a data or the information, churning and processing machines. If it is done, life is ought to become too miserable very soon, and it simply means that the life has been grossly mistaken, and is misdirected. Be a sport for the life, as it is a very brief life. Do those things in the life, which truly matter to you, otherwise do not do. Sleep like a baby. Stop any overthinking. Keep hands folded or joined together as in the Namaskara stance, and sit and join the feet, as doing so frequently, takes away all stresses, anxieties and worries. Anxieties and worries are physiologically and psychologically created, therefore, these can only be annihilated by natural physiological and psychological ways. Happiness is a psychological creation only, and nothing else.

CHAPTER THREE

Sufferings

Do not suffer in the life. Learn, not to suffer the failures. Also, be careful about the success, subtly turning into the sufferings. Always, suffering makes the life full of tragedies, and converts the being into a tragedian. Try experiencing the real happiness, the inner happiness. Manage the life. Learn the life engineering skills. Defeat the death in order to live the life. Defeat all fears in order to be happy in the journey of life. Death is the biggest fear of majority of beings. Why to fear the death, when there is a definite reunion for all without exception. Life only begins, when one goes beyond the death. It is natural to suffer the failures and the sufferings, but it is painful to find that beings also suffer their successes and the happiness. Suffering is the perception, discordant with the reality, as in reality, there is nothing like suffering. Find some meaning in every suffering in order to live the life. There is no suffering, which sans its solution, similar to, as every lock has some key. Suffering is the part of life training. There is no victory without sufferings. Life is not only about the happiness, but it is also about the sufferings. Suffering is the teacher of the life. Sufferings create challenges for the life. A being, which fears the sufferings, is already suffering the fear, and is a living dead, a zombie. Be fearless. Fear is death. Be brave. There is no or lesser suffering in reality, as compared with, that in the imaginations. Learn converting sufferings into the pleasures. Be peaceful, i.e. peace from inside. Draw power and energy from the universe; look up, at the heavens, stretch your arms, and embrace the space, and the blessing, power and energy will descend. Feel the infinity outside, and also inside. Sufferings do not hold us, but, we hold the sufferings. Suffering is a gift in reality. Enjoy every moment of the life. This too shall pass. Sufferings strengthen the soul. Sufferings build the character. Develop resilience to outlive the sufferings. Success paves its ways through sufferings only. In essence, there is nothing like loss or less or never, in the life. Do not live in any kind of bondage, as for every being, there is already enough freedom, given by the God, in his or her journey of the life. Do not suffer the freedom. Attachments may create sufferings, therefore, work on these. In the show and the game of the life, we all are alone. We come alone at the time of birth, and also, go alone, at the time of death. Get attached to the nature and the God, and all sufferings will vanish in the thin air. Sufferings are outcomes of the negative plays of the mind, created in order to trouble the being. Do not let the mind (memory and intellect) to work against you; rather, use these consciously for self-growth, progress and evolution, and for you. Success and failure, happiness and sufferings, are organically linked to one another. With every perceptible suffering, try deepening faith and belief, more and more in the forces of the nature, the universe, and the God, and one day, there will be no more sufferings, but only happiness in the life, in every moment and the everything all around, throughout the life. Use every experience of the life, whether good or bad, it does not matter, for transforming the self now, making the self, better than before, as it is the very purpose and the design of the life, for every being, without exception. Happiness does not come, but is created.

CHAPTER FOUR

Problems And Solutions

Beings search for solutions to the problems of the life throughout their life. Struggling to find the solution, takes away the happiness. Life is a collection of problems, and the problems are the part of it. There will be many challenges and issues, which every being has to face in his or her journey of life. There is no exception to it. If there are no problems, there will be no life. A dead has no problems. Therefore, do not be afraid of the problems of the life. The God has designed the life like this only i.e. full of problems with overt and covert solutions and answers, for each one of us, with no exceptions, even for the incarnations. In the life, there are more problems that the comforts. Problems and solutions are the two created perceptions in the brain, and basically a play of the mind. Mind tests us, teases us, by creating the negative side of everything. Conquer the mind, and all the problems will vanish. Mind is the seat of all problems. Do Yoga and meditation. Let, the problems of the life do not stop the happiness in the life. For every lock, always there is a key. Many problems in the life can be solved. Whereas, many other problems may be difficult to solve, therefore learn to face such problems, as facing is the key to the solution of such problems. The problems, which cannot be solved, have to be faced. In the game of life, become strong and stronger in order to face tough and tougher problems. This is what the life teaches to each one of us. We do not always need advice(s) of others, but, many times, we need someone to hold us, listen to us, and simply understand us. Always be grateful and positive, and even more especially during the difficult and troubled times of the life, as doing so, uplifts the being. A saviour comes and saves us. It is the design of the life. The invisible helping hand of the God appears. Maintenance of the mind, the body and the emotions is very critical for managing the situations of the life. If one is sad and miserable, then he or she will be the part of the problem, on the contrary, if one is happy and exuberant, then he or she will be the part of the solution. The latter being remains unaffected by the problems of the life. Always remember that one day, every being dies, therefore, act consciously, wisely and meaningfully. Live the life happily, without worries, stresses and anxieties. Manage the life. Manage the body. Manage the mind well with proper thoughts. Empower the spirit inside. Body is intelligent. Every cell of the body has memory and the intelligence. Cell works, as per the thoughts. Even the cells within the body fight back with the negative thoughts and the emotions, and the effects created thereof, to the extent they can. Cells and the body must be used properly for advantages in the life. All experiences of the life are generated from within. Life is not outside, but inside. All outer experiences are inner projections. The only solution to all the problems is to simplify all the problems, and their solutions get available. Life is too simple. Do not develop such an attitude, which makes the life and its associated things complex. Complexity is created in the mind. Keep the mind silent, and the answers to the problems, simply break through. Try to live with the problems, cope with it, and endure it. Always give time to time. Have patience. During the tougher times of the life, trust, faith and the belief work in magical manner and ways. Nothing here in this creation happens, before its destined time, and at the right the place (space). Stay with the questions without agitation and reactions. Try to make the life effortless. Create understanding for everything in the life. Success, name, money and fame are too short and purely temporary. Do not be wannabe. You are the best, as you are. Life is all about the struggles. By rewiring the brain, we can change the trajectory of the life, and destiny of the life. When in the problem, first sit down and become silent, listen to the silence, i.e. the inner voice, and the answer comes, as given by the soul supported by the universe. Silence is never empty. Silence carries all the answers of the life and its associated things, situations and circumstances. All the problems of the life have their solutions. Life is a package of problems and solutions, happiness and displeasure, success and failure, and birth and death. Outside in the nature, there is day and night, white and black, and good and bad. Everything has its dual. Solutions are found, only in the presence of peace and the silence, and not in the presence of mental noise. Practise the silence in order to make the life free of problems. Become buddha, i.e. the enlightened being, and not the buddhu. Life becomes what we make it, and how we make it. Worrying does not solve tomorrow's problems, but only take away today's peace. Try living beyond all thoughts, emotions and the feelings. Live beyond the blood, in the biggest family. Stay connected to the inner self, and the happiness will always be experienced.

CHAPTER FIVE

Success And Failure

Success and failures are perceived outcomes of various life activities and the processes. Both, success and failure are never final. Self-belief and the hard work bring success. Love what you do. There are many unsuccessful years, and then, the success comes. Success follows the failure. Follow your passion. Keep moving in the journey of life. Keep going. Live in enthusiasm. Life teaches continuously, therefore, never stop learning. Failure should not define and stop us, and nor the success. Life is a continuous journey. Family, friends, relations, neighbours are the co-passengers of this journey of life. Who we are? From where, we come before the birth? Where we go after the death? Why we are here on earth? Is there a God? These are a few of many other intriguing questions of the life, and the answers to these, a being keeps on finding his or her whole life. Answers are given by the universe during meditation. An enlightened being understands the design of the life, and also, the whole creation. Your time will come. Success brings joy and happiness. Failure paves the way for success, and comes with certain learning. Success and failure are only the dramatic events, the outcomes. Success and failure are based on the Law of Probability. Either a thing will discretely happen or discretely not happen. If success does not happen, failure will occur, and if, failure does not occur, success will happen. Being alone is responsible for both, success and failure. Always remind yourself that, if mind can conceive something, then it can be surely be created in the physical world. Mind cannot create the things beyond the Akashic Intellligence. All intelligence pervades through the entire universe, and is known as the Akashic Intelligence. Success does not bring happiness; rather, it is the happiness, which brings success. Every single work, which seems to be difficult, and sometimes even impossible, is that, which has not been even attempted. Success and failure are materialistic outcomes of effort(s), whereas the happiness is the spiritual outcome of effort(s). Ignorance and confidence both are needed for achieving success in the life. Do all simple and common things, in uncommonly ways; as it is only the mantra of success. In the journey of life, seemingly difficult roads lead to the beautiful destinations. It is not just about the ideas, but all about making the ideas to happen through planning and actions, which brings success, name and fame, and the wealth. Failure is the key to success, rather a part of the success only. Subtly, failure is success in progress. Heed the lessons of failure. Learn to convert the failure into the success. Actually, there are no such things like success and failure in the universe. Do not get defined by success or failure in the life. Learn to deal with toxic beings. If there is no pain, there will be no gain. Life is not simple. Learn to handle the failures with stout hearts. Dedicate with utmost purity of the heart, both success and failures to the God, put the life at his feet, and he (the God) will completely takeover, and give you the happiness. God is our constant companion in the journey of the life, then why to worry. All, which comes in the way of journey of the life, is God's design for us, which is always best for us. God is our real parent, the spiritual parent. Success, failure and happiness, all are given by the God only, therefore, demand success and happiness from the God.

CHAPTER SIX

Faith, Hope And Courage

We do not grow, when things are easy, but, when we face the challenges. It is not "the difficult", which stops from trying, but it is not trying, which makes the things difficult. Difficulties exist only in perception, which is unreal. Perception is not always real. Hold the faith that things will get better soon, and they will. It might be raining cats and dog now, but it cannot remain so for ever. Give time, its time. Give space, its space. Hope is, what makes one to see the light, despite all the darkness. Not to fear of, is the courage. It is the courage to begin, which brings the success in the life. Aura shrinks and expands in proportion to the courage. Courage is grace under pressure, while performing a daunting or a challenging task. Faith makes the impossible possible, and thus, brings joy and the happiness. Faith is all about the God doing, what is just right. Faith gives an inner strength. It also creates a balance in the life. When doubt dies, faith is born. Faith is unquestioning belief. Hope is a dream in motion. Hope makes the impossible possible like the faith. Even the last thread of hope is quite powerful. If there is a hope, there will be life. It is the hope, which makes all things to work in this creation. If there is love also, things will become easier. Hope is the gift of the God, given to each one of us, and it exists, even if, one is at the lowest point of his or her life. Hope is the basis of whole creation. Faith, hope and courage are the characteristics of the soul. We all have been given this life by the God, because we all are strong enough to live it. We get in the life, what we have courage to ask for. Courage is the decision. The unconquered fear becomes a barrier for the happiness. Courage resists the fear, and gives the mastery of the fear. Nothing can substitute the experiences, therefore, have courage, be brave and take the risks. Life is a collection of experiences. Opportunities in the life are created by the God. The toughest times of the life are the bigger opportunities thrown before us by the God. Happiness lies on the other end of the life. Happiness is always internal and never external, like peace. External happiness is simply a farce. Always trust the God. We are not alone in the journey of the life. There are many God sent spirits, which accompany each one of us, all throughout the journey of the life. At the time of birth, there are many spirits, which await our arrival in this physical world, similarly, at the time of death, there are many spirits, which arrive here to take us away. This arrangement of the spirits and their presence in the life has been made by the God, in order to keep the help available, whenever needed, and become happy eventually. Happiness is an experience. Try experiencing this experience all the time in the life. Trust the God in the times of uncertainty, difficulties, pains and the miseries. Even if everything has gone, keep the faith, faith in the self, faith in the nature, faith in the universe, and finally, the faith in the God. Who we are, not even a speck of the dust, the insignificant one, in this vast creation. Do not over define and over emphasise yourself. Everything was perfect, is perfect, and will be perfect. It is a constantly changing creation; it is such a design, the wonderful design. There should be no room for anything, which is negative or painful. Learn to live in the happiness, peace and the joy. Stop worrying, give it to the God. Do not fear any outcome. Do not fear the evil. Even, do not fear, when walking through the shadow of death, as the God is with us there also. Life cannot sustain without him (the God). Trust God's timings. God is working for us without stopping, without sleeping. No being is a mistake. We all have been sent here by the God with certain purpose. For instance, the purpose may not be working, but simply observing the things, beings and the world around. Life without purpose is a far bigger tragedy than the death. A life, which sans the purpose, has no destiny and precision. If one has no purpose, he would not have born. The God knows all about us, each one of us, and also, about everything, in this his creation. God knew everything about us, even much before, we were born. God allowed our birth, as there was some purpose. Have good thoughts. Keep making best possible efforts. Rest, leave everything to the God. All have to go the God, some day. Anything, which is physical, is an illusion and just temporary. Only, which is spiritual, is real and the permanent. True love is spiritual and permanent. Do not destroy the planet in the name of knowledge, progress and the development, else a day, everything will be gone, including the happiness. He, who destroys himself, is the biggest fool. The inner peace, satisfaction and the pleasure are only real, which bring real happiness. External happiness is no happiness. Do meditation and yoga. Laugh without restraints. Keep smiling. Win the hearts. Smile has its own charm. Have faith in the self and the God, hope for the best, have courage to speak and do which is just right, and the happiness will descend. Happiness is a blessing, and the universe does not give it to ever being, but it is accessible to all. Control the emotions. Put the God first, and trust his plans. God tests us. Use the power of prayer.

CHAPTER SEVEN

Growth And Excellence

Nothing is useless in this creation. Every being and everything here in the existence serve a different unique purpose. Believe yourself for all your abilities. You can. Never ever give up in the journey of life, no matter what. When we give up, there is no growth. Never quit. Challenges and struggles grow our roots deep and deeper for our growth and excellence. Everything in the life happens at the right time with the approval of the nature and the life. Be patient. Be the player when in action, be the witness when waiting for the outcome(s) of the action(s), and show the humility and express the gratitude, whatever is the outcome(s). Success and failure are the creations of the mind, and nothing here in the life is too lasting. Life has no set pattern and the format. Every being is simply unique. Also, every being is alone here. We are energies. This creation is the result of a constant play of energies. Cosmos is energy. God is energy. Energy exchange creates the karma. Thought is energy. Action is energy. There is life energy, mind energy and spirit energy. Everything is just energy. Love is a positive energy. Hate is a negative energy. Every emotion is energy. It is not about what happens from the outside, but all about, how one deals with it, from the inside, as it changes the life positively, into the growth and excellence. Growth starts with discomfort and the agitation of mind. Make the agitating mind to settle down with work. Work done in the right direction will quell all agitations of the mind. Growth is optional, but very necessary in the life. It is not only about the physical growth, but also about the religious and spiritual growth. Keep adapting constantly, revising and changing you. Changes in the environment are inevitable, as such is the design of the cosmos. Birth is a change, death is also a change, but the core (soul) always exists and beyond any change. Soul always exists, which is the only true identity of any being. Inside growth brings the outside growth. Perseverance brings the growth. Every simple thing had been hard initially. Growth brings freedom also. Constantly check and correct yourself. Excellence is an attitude. Excellence is a constant pursuit of perfection. Make the excellence a habit. Autograph every work done with the excellence; it will bring in immense happiness. Growth and excellence both are constant processes. Perfection brings growth and excellence both. Perfection has no set definition; just do the things with best of abilities and with full interest. Growth and excellence are the results of always striving to do better. Keep learning in the life. If learning stops, growth will stop. Success is about "having", but growth and excellence are about "being". Desire for growth and excellence bring in divine fulfilments in one's life. Never lose exuberance and enthusiasm. The key to happiness is growth and constantly working on the path of progress towards the excellence.

CHAPTER EIGHT

Be The Original

Be the original, as only original is valued and appreciated, and not its copies. We are original. Do not follow the others; rather follow the self, i.e. the instinct. Only take the inspiration from those, who are worthy of it. Live the life as the original, and follow your own nature and passion(s). Overcome the fear of being judged by others. Only, the self-judgement about the self, matters in one's life. Remove all the masks and make-up. Be the pure soul, peaceful and happy soul. The God has already sent us as the most beautiful unique entity of this existence, which is his sole creation. We all are very different. We all are individuals. God has created us to be different and unique. We all are his (God's) individuated energies. We all have different life's purposes. Being different is being attractive and beautiful. Our looks, nature, likes and dislikes etc., all are quite different. It is very simple to be happy, but quite difficult to be simple. Simplicity is the originality. Simplicity is the real greatness. Be straight to yourself. Listen to the soul. Soul is older than the heart and wiser than the mind. One cannot make right decisions all the time, but can definitely learn from the wrong ones every time. Stand up for what is right, even if, you are standing alone. Find out, where we fit, and do that only, and be there. Do not fear anything.

Start and end the day with the name of the God. Happiness is a journey, and not any destination, do not postpone this journey. Be always blissed out, on cloud none. Be happy for being you. We are we. We all are best at something. Do a thing, as if, the God has made us for doing that thing only. Recognise the self and identify self-strengths. Beings pass their lives, but do not know, who they are, therefore, discover the self. Discovering the self is the discovery of the God, and the discovery of the happiness. It is the discovery of the truth. Do good in order to receive the good. The Law of Karma is the Law of Cause and Effect, i.e. action and reaction. As we sow, so shall we reap. Become stoned and insensitive to all those, who judge you negatively, and discourage you. Listen to every being but do not get affected by every being. Do not let your self-confidence limit you. Believe in the self. Become physically, mentally and emotionally strong. Live on cloud eleven. Do not copy or imitate others. We are "the best", as we are. There is always beauty in variety, and monotony in similarity. Interestingly, no two things in this creation are exactly same, something will be different. If they exist separately, there is definitely something, which is quite distinct. Karma makes the entities different from one another. Karma is energy impression. In this creation, there is electromagnetic energy. Spirits are made from love and the light. Light is electrical energy. Matter, which associates itself with the energy, in order to create a physical body, is bound by the magnetic energy. It is the electromagnetic energy in the space outside, and also inside, which pervades all through. There is another space inside the physical body. However, the inside space and the outside space are not different, but all the same. What we are, is the state of our electromagnetic energy. Happiness emerges from a certain state of this electromagnetic energy. Energy makes the matter to work. Spirit makes the body to work. Things, which are non-physical, are energy, and the things, which are physical, are matter or the material. We all are unique blend of energy and the matter or the material. In a given birth and the journey of the life, the energy and the matter or the material cannot be changed. It can only be changed in another new association of energy and the matter, in the next life i.e. rebirth. No two beings have the same energy and matter properties, and their composition. The proportions of the energy and the matter, make us, what we are, our attitudes, moods, health, personality, mind, physical, mental and spiritual strengths and the endurance. We are reflection or the image of our past. Our present life and associated states are effects of our previous life(s). What we do now in this life, will affect the future of this life, and will go to the next life. There are ample learning and improvement opportunities provided by the universe to every being in every journey of the life. By conscious use of choices and the freewill, the process of learning and self-improvement can be improved more and more. Learning and the improvements made, create impressions on the soul, which travel to the next life, i.e. life after the death and the next physical life. Thus, we are born with the traits (Samskara), which we had brought from the previous life(s). Many things in the life are simply a done deal, or the fait accompli, i.e. fixed and irrevocable, irreversible or immutable. Trying to change the self or complaining about the present form is interfering by intent in the works of the God. Live the life without complaints and making the judgements. It is an illusory world. Everything is continuously changing here. Nothing and no being is fixed and going to stay in the present form. The design of the life is completely known to the God, and partly understood by few enlightened beings. Majority simply passes the life in confusion, frustration and in mind's created miseries. All trials and tribulations are creations of the mind. Manage the mind. Use it, for you, and not against you. Similarly, use the intellect and the intelligence, for you, and not against you. If we live original, everything will happen the right way. Be simple, humble, loving and caring, and then, the originality will stay, and the happiness will simply follow.

CHAPTER NINE

Good Spouse

Good spouse is one of the bigger sources of happiness in the life. Marriages are made in the heaven and solemnised on the earth. Spouse is the real soulmate. Soulmates even live together in the Spirit World. Not every husband or the wife here on the earth is a soulmate. Who will be the spouse, is the matter of one's karma. There may be role reversal, i.e. husband becoming the wife, and wife become the husband, in future rebirths. The purpose of the life is to learn through the experiences, all sorts of experiences. We all assume nearly all forms of relationships in various lives. The true spouse loves, just the way one is. Our attitudes and personalities are different, yet with certain beings, our compatibility happens to be the best. For electric current to flow, there is a requirement of two distinct potentials. Or, for the water to flow there is a requirement of two distinct levels. And this, flow of electric current, then brings the life to the electrical circuit. Similarly, our different personalities are necessary to create the families, relations, friends, society, states, nations, world, and this universe. Fall in love with yourself first. The two great days of life are day of birth and day of discovering, "why". Be strong but not rude, be proud but not arrogant, be humble but not timid, and be kind but not weak. Remain happy. Work hard.

Success comes by consistent work, and not by working occasionally. Learn to live. Give love and respect to others, and same will come back to you. Living in the past and observing the others prevent the happiness. Physical gain or loss in the life is no gain or loss. Death is not the loss. The greatest loss is what dies within, while living. A good spouse understands you, and your most of the things. He or she, who does not understand the silence, will never be able to understand the words. Difficult times and the challenges in the life are God's design for us, and their purpose is not to destroy, but to promote and increase the strength. Manage the mind. Train the self to let go things, which create any fear of loss. During the journey of life, at every time, something falls away and something beautiful is on the way, and awaiting us. Affection brings perfection. Try connecting with other's innate goodness. Do not judge the other. Do not always correct his or her mistakes. There are ample opportunities in the life, opportunities to learn, and opportunities to grow and succeed. Learn the art of identifying these opportunities. Sit still. Work on the mind and the body. Settle the mind, emotions and the energy. Do not doubt the self. Work hard in the life. Make the things to happen. Love yourself. Say no to the things which sap you away, drain your energy, and make feel burdened. Every action may not bring the happiness, but there will be no happiness, if there is no action. Only during the darkest moments of the life, we learn, and strive to focus on the light, with all our abilities. Best life is not found in the comfort, but in the struggle, and striving to find for, what we believe in. Life gets its meaning, only when there are challenges, defeats, failures, success and the progress. Life has a very simple design. However, the complexity of the thoughts and confusion of the actions, make the life complicated. A being can only change his or her life, and no other being can. Life is a continuous journey. First step of the journey is very necessary in order to make the journey of thousands miles to happen. Life does not need many things for its happiness, and all the things are within, in the way of thinking. Be happy in the every moment of the life, for these moments only make create the life. God gives the life, but it is created by us. Life is not a problem. Life is a reality to be experienced. Many failures of the life, simply fail to turn into the success, as efforts were given up at the very verge of the success. Wishing or knowing is simply not enough, but actions are always needed for achieving everything in the life, and to make the things to happen. Failures build the character. Do not let any failure stop us. We learn more from the failure than the success. To be happy, is the sole purpose of the life, and the art to be happiness is to be satisfied with whatever we have. Nothing bothers more than the self-mind. Being deeply loved, gives the strength, whereas, loving deeply, gives courage. A good spouse helps to grow and inspires to "be". Love of spouse is stronger than the death. A good spouse is the gift of the God for bringing happiness in the life.

CHAPTER TEN

A Good Family

Good children, and the good spouse, make a good family. A good family is the one of the bigger sources of happiness in the life. Spend your time with yourself, and with your family, and you will start liking, which you really are. Always energise your family, and the home. Be the spark. A Good family makes "the house", a "home", a beautiful home. Use the power of mind to solve the problems of the life. No problem is really a problem; rather it is just another experience. Situations and circumstances, as the problems of life, are false creations of the mind. Manage the mind to present the solutions, and not the problems. Stop the chatters of the mind. Negative thoughts are the biggest source of problems of life. Have positive thinking, as it is very powerful. Do yoga and meditation to silent the disturbed mind. A family is like a tree, where we all grow, like the branches of the tree in different directions, yet connected to a common root. When there are storms in the life, and life is mid waters, good family acts like a life jacket. A good family is one of the great blessings in the life. A good life begins with a good family. Love never ends in a good family. Love is the source of everything, and also, the basis of the whole creation. God is love, and love is God. Family is not just "a thing", but the "everything" in the life. A good family is one's circle of strength, which is founded on faith, and joined by the pure unconditional love. Families are created in the Spirit World, and the members of the family, allotted for a given life, descend to the Physical World, to live together, and pay off and settle their karma. Family is the set of beings, with whom, we have maximum due karmic settlements. No being appears in the life, without having a due karmic settlement. One's family is his or her best team, where, no being, gets left behind, or is forgotten. A family needs not to be perfect, but remain united. True riches of the life, are one's good family and friends. Mother is the angel in the family. She is the pillar of the family. A good family is an assurance, and also, insurance for love and care. Create a balance between the work and the family. Family affects the life, more than the work. Create a high vibrational power. Vibrations directly affect the life. Good thoughts attract good quality of life. What we think, we become, and happens in the life. Life needs a happy state of the mind, beautiful relations and loving relationships, good health, and a beautiful world around. We are the creators of our own destinies. All these things, we have to create-bring into our life. Create a positive self-image. Clean the karma on the daily basis. Learn to deal with the toxic beings, and safeguard your family from such beings. A toxic being is one, whose behaviour adds negativity, and upsets your life. Do not expect anything from any being and still love them in order to remain happy in the life. Let us not contribute in emotional pollution. Love and value yourself. Remain stable. Experience the God. Attract positive energies. No one can hurt us, except our self. Carry attitude of gratitude, as gratitude carries the power to change the destiny. Increase the willpower. Realise the self, and increase the level of the consciousness, and the world around will change, and become too beautiful. Be neutral and just. Be equitable. Discipline the self. What we are, our family becomes like that, therefore, be good, so as to have a good family. Happiness is an experience, more internal and less external. A good family is always a happy family, and acts as the biggest source of happiness in the life.

CHAPTER ELEVEN

Good Deeds

Keep doing good deeds in the life. Good deeds are the security deposits of the life. Whenever severe storms hit the life badly, these good deeds already done prove to be a kayak, which rescues us from devastation, destruction and ruination. Do not become greedy in the life. Understand the difference between the need and the greed. Greed comes between need and want. The quality of life cannot be raised without raising the texture of thoughts, and deepening the depth of understanding. Whatever good we get in the life, is all due to the good deeds done, either presently or in the past. Life can give us lots of beautiful and rich friends, but only true friends can give us beautiful and rich life. Do good to others, as it surely comes back in many unexpected and inexplicable ways. Learn how to adjust with other beings, and when to void the beings. Actions are effective than the intentions. Good deeds leave a trail, and imprints on the hearts of other beings. Good deeds are always devoid of expectations. Good deeds create a harmony in the existence. Do not do good for show-off. Keep the circle around, very positive. Always speak good words. Always think good thoughts. Every good deed is a good prayer. A good deed is the best offering to the God. God makes the good deeds very easy to do, only for the blessed beings.

Good deeds create goodwill. Good deeds remove the darkness and brighten up the world around. Goodness is the characteristic of the soul. Sometimes being soft can be strong, as grass is all that remains standing after the storm. Always remain light by removing all emotional baggage. Energise your home with peace. Control the mind to increase the will power. Stop all negative thoughts. Karma Yoga, also known as Karma Marga, is one of the four classical spiritual paths. Karma Yoga is based on the "Yoga of Action". Karma Yoga aims at selfless action as a way to the perfection. Jñāna Yoga, also known as Jñāna Mārga, is the classical path for Moksha. Moksha is the release from the cycle of rebirth. Jñāna Yoga emphasizes the "path of knowledge", i.e. the "path of self-realization". The Jñāna Yoga is a spiritual practice, which pursues knowledge with questions like, "Who am I, "What am I", "Why I am born", "What is the purpose of life", "What is life", "What is Karma", "Is there a God", "Who created this universe", "How this universe was created" etc.. Raja Yoga aims to achieve control over the mind and emotions. Bhakti Yoga, also known as Bhakti Marga is the spiritual path or the spiritual practice, which focuses on loving devotion towards a deity. Good deeds are seeds of a tree, which produces sweet fruits, i.e. the good outcomes. Deeds are karma. One's life is his or her karma. We are the source of our own life. Physical, mental and life energies control is very necessary for a good life. Deeds create memories, and memories create the deeds. Sharpen the senses in order to perceive deep and deeper. A deeper perception creates the consciousness. Deeds must be consciously done, and let the subconscious and the unconscious minds and memories, do not affect the journey of the life, but it is not easy.

Subconscious mind is very powerful, and so is the unconscious mind. Without rigorous Yoga and meditation, it is not possible to access the subconscious and unconscious minds. Good deeds are the source of all happiness in the life.

CHAPTER TWELVE

A Good Life

A well lived life is a good life. When we are thankful for all that we have, we are being rewarded more and more by the universe. Nothing is sweeter than to think well of the others. Treating others with respect, costs nothing, but earns everything. The love of the family and the admiration by the friends is much more important than the wealth and the privileges in the life. Life smiles at us, when we are happy, but salutes us, when we make others happy. In the context of life, unlike the language, open and close are not two opposite words, as we get "open" to those beings, to which we get "close". The quality of life depends on our abilities to manage the situations, which arise during the journey of life. The journey of the life was never simple and straight, even for the messengers or the incarnations of the God. Never measure the achievements of the life by the physical possessions. Measure it by the hearts you have touched, the number of smiles, which you have created, and the love, which has been showered and shared. No regrets, only lessons. No worries, only acceptance. No expectations, only gratitude. These are the simple and amazing secrets of a good life. Life is short. Dreams do not have expiration date. If did not get what aspired, take a deep breath and try again. Every day of the life should be beautiful. Do not complain, cry and fret about the past, as it already over. Also, do not take any stress about the future, as it has not come yet. Live in the present, and make it, as beautiful, as meaningful and as memorable, as possible. To make the difference in your life, and also, in the life of the others, one does not need to be brilliant or rich or beautiful or perfect, rather one just needs to care about the self and the others. Apologising does not mean that you are wrong, and the other being is right, but it only means that you value your relationship with that being, more than your ego. Silence is the best answer to a being, which does not value your words. Be sharp. Be smart. Do not evaluate the things by their face values. For happiness in the life, lead a simple life. Have good thoughts. Actions must be good. Life is a continuous journey. Life is a continuous celebration. Birth is a celebration; similarly death is also a celebration. There is not even a single reason to feel sorrow for something, or to repent about something, in the life. Things come in the life, and fo awaty from the life. Live a life of detachment. This detachment does not mean, become rude, or insensitive or indifferent. In the journey of the life, always remember the God. Do Dhyana Yoga. Dhyana Yoga is also known as Aṣṭāṅgayoga (eight-fold mystic perfection). Dhyana Yoga is given by the sage Patanjali. In Dhyana Yoga, the practitioner relieves him or herself from all the engagements with the help of regulative processes of meditation, concentration, certain sitting postures, and by blocking the movements of internal circulation of air. Make the God, a consciously chosen companion in the journey of life, and then, the life will become light and airy. When we belong to the God, then everything thing, whether physical and non-physical with us, also belongs to the God only.

Notice the beings, which make efforts to stay with us in our life. Life is full of beauty, just notice it. Our children, family, relations, friends, etc., all are created by the God, as per our design of the life. Every being's design of life is unique; therefore, never compare your life with the life of the others. We live with our children, family, relations, friends etc., for certain duration, for gaining certain experiences of the life, as per our karma. Karma is the basis of everything. Karma is the memory. Karma is the energy. Good karma means good energy, and the bad karma means bad energy. Be strong. The purpose of the life is just to remain happy. Happiness is never external, but always internal. Happiness is the secret to all the beauty, and there is no beauty without happiness. See the good side of everything in order to bring happiness in the life. A happy life is a process, a direction, and not a state or a destination. Use the things, and not the beings. Love the beings, and not the things. Lead a conscious life. Exercise the power to choose prudently, i.e. what to accept, and what to let go, in the life. We are just given the life by the God, and it is we, who make it "a good life". Smile, dream and laugh, as these give a meaning to the life, and bring the happiness. Have faith. Keep trying and never give up. There is no problem without a solution, rather many solutions. Stay as youthful as kids. Be simple like the kids. Life needs not to be perfect, in order to be good and happy. Life is always wonderful. Life is always good. God's sent every life, every moment of the life, every situation of the life, are just perfect the way they are. Do not compare the self with the others, as what you are, is not the other being. God has created the variety knowingly. There are no two exactly same things or beings in this entire creation. Everything is just good, and also perfect, as it is. Beauty lies in the variety. Similarity brings the monotony. Explore the secrets of the life, in order to explore life's goodness, and also, the happiness. Keep moving. Keep making yourself from simple to simpler, and you will find that your understanding about the life increases. It is one step towards the enlightenment. Life otherwise, is a big trap, and do not get entangled in it. Live like the Sun or the Moon, like a river or an ocean, like a mountain, like a tree, or like a bird. Draw all inspiration from the nature. Live free. Live to give. Share the things. Sharing is caring. Free yourself from the trap of the mind. Manage the mind. Live to inspire the others. We are the gods.

CHAPTER THIRTEEN

Earthly Life And The Afterlife

We all experience a certain earthly life here. Life is lived and experienced. No two beings have same earthly life. There is a definite afterlife. No two beings have same afterlife. Afterlife is the life, which exists after the death. The afterlife is also known as the "Life after Death" or the "World to Come". Life is ad infinitum. Life is a continuous journey. Eternity does not start with the death, but, we all are already into the eternity, now and here. Birth and death are two major events of the life process. It is the Physical World, where we live presently. After death, we go to the Spirit World. Here, in the Physical World, a being is made up of matter and energy, whereas, in the Spiritual World, a being is only made up of energy. Before the birth, we all remain in the energy form, and after the death, again, we get the energy form. In the Physical World, in the earthly life, there are more pains than the pleasures, as it is a test life. In the Spirit World, in the afterlife, there is no pain, but only pleasure. Here, in the earthly life, we are spirits in the body form, whereas, in the afterlife, we are only spirits, and there are no physical bodies. There are many earths in this existence. There are many universes in this existence, known as the multiverse. There are many suns and many moons in this existence. There are many invisible beings, which keep watching us every moment at every place. To everything, there is a season. Immediately after the death, beings get a feeling like a baby in the mother's womb, i.e. wrapped and cuddled by the mother nature, feeling safe and secure, feeling great comfort and a sense of completion, and utter peace. Life flashes before the eyes immediately after the death. Death is an illusion. Time is a big landscape, where, past, present and future, all three, coexist. Birth and the death exist together. In the earthly life, there are choices, but in the afterlife, there are no choices. So, choose to live happy here during the earthly life. Present is carried forward to the future, similar to, as the past is carried forward to the present, therefore "happiness", if exists in the presence, will be carried forward to the future. A happy earthly life is a guarantee to a happy afterlife. In the afterlife, beings live with their tendencies. The state of death greatly affects the quality of the afterlife, so die in peace, and then, peace will prevail over the entire duration of the afterlife. Some part of mind passes on to the other side with the spirit of being into his or her afterlife, but this part of the mind is non-discriminatory. Lead a halcyon earthly life, as it will create an idyllic afterlife. Here, in the earthly life, things are in the conscious control of the beings, but there in the afterlife, things are not in the conscious control of the beings. When we see our loved ones in the afterlife, it is more loving, than on the earth. Here during the earthly life and later there in the afterlife, we live according to our spiritual elements, at suitable levels. There are many levels of existence or living, both in the earthly life and also in the afterlife. All the beings do not live at the same level during their earthly life and afterlife. These are the levels of understanding, consciousness and awareness, sensitivity, peace, calm and composure, need and greed, knowledge, religiosity, and the happiness. Do not look for happiness somewhere else, or in some other moment, or from some other being; rather create it now and here, by self-help and efforts and directed actions. Eliminate all your fears. Work on the mind. Trust the power of faith and belief. Believe in your strengths. Believe in the power of thoughts. Happiness is so amazing, that it does not matter, whether it is yours or not.

CHAPTER FOURTEEN

Freewill And The Choices

Freewill and the choices totally affect the life. Freewill is the power or ability to make self-decisions about the life, rather than being controlled by any outside influence. Freewill is exercised by the discriminatory mind. Freewill option is only available in the physical life in the Physical World, i.e. on the earth, and not available in the Spiritual World. There in the Spiritual World, beings lead their lives with their tendencies, as the mind, which goes along with the spirit, is non-discriminatory. Where there is a tendency, there will be no choice. Tendency is something that a being or thing usually does. Tendency is the way of behaving. Exercising the freewill and the choices, have a direct and full bearing on the trajectory of the life. For happiness in the life, freewill must be exercised to make the correct choices. Life always presents multiple options, and there is always a best one. The option chosen affects the life. Life is a matter of choice(s). You never know, which footstep will bring a good twist in the life, so keep walking. Happiness comes, when it is most unexpected. Birth and death are in the control of the existence. Birth is a start as well as an end. Death is an end as well as a beginning. One can chose to be a victor or a victim in any situation or circumstance. The lessons of the life come along with the freewill and the choices. Use the freewill and the choices for love, goodness and joy. Freewill is the freedom to do right things. Freewill determines the fate. The universe does not interfere with our choices, and this exactly is the freewill. God gave us freewill so that we may create our destinies. Freewill and the choices, if not exercised properly, make create new karma. Do not create any new karma for salvation, nirvana and moksha. Salvation is getting saved from the power of evil, danger, disaster etc.. Nirvana is the state of peace and the happiness, which is achieved after giving up personal desires. Moksha is the transcendental state, which is attained as a result of being released from the cycle of rebirth, impelled by the Law of Karma. In order to not to create any new karma, do not kill birds or animals or plants or any other being, adopt nonviolence, do not interfere in other's life, do not judge others, and do Dhyana or the Meditation. Past is the destiny. Future is the freewill. Freewill is the choice with every experience of the life. We all are connected with the cosmos and the infinity, and this connection brings along, the freedom, i.e. freewill and the choices. Freewill has the power to modify the chain of karma. Freewill acts in the present moment, and may create freedom, if exercised properly, or the bondage, if not exercised properly, in the moments to come. Freewill and the choices made in the past become karma. Happiness depends upon karma, and karma depends on freewill and choices, therefore, happiness depends on freewill and the choices. There is a cosmic will, which is like an order, and happens, even if we try preventing it. However, freewill is the decision to be made. One's existence is the cosmic will, but his or her actions, and the decisions, are the matter of his or her freewill and the choices. Everything is not predestined in the life. Cosmic will becomes laws of the universe. Life's framework is based on the cosmic will. Cosmic will cannot be altered, but using the cosmic forces to one's life's advantage is the right exercise of freewill and the choices. Nature is here to support us always. Nature is full of compassion. Freewill and the choices are empowered by the thought. Freewill and the choices should always have the components of devotion and the love, devotion and love towards the God, and towards the works undertaken. Replacing "have to do" with "want to do" definitely yields good results, as it is caused by the conscious exercise of freewill and the choices. Spiritual laws like the Law of Karma, Law of Dharma, Law of Giving, Law of Intention and Desire etc. are the guiding compass of our life. Law of Karma is the Law of Karuna, in essence. Karuna (in Hindi) means compassion or mercy. Law of Karma is for the purpose of self-growth and evolution. My life is result of my karma. Determinism, and Freewill and the Choices, both exist in the life, in certain proportions. Determinism means that events and action are determined by the causes, which are not governed by the freewill. Determinism is the cosmic will. Happiness is using the freewill and power to make the happy choices, agreeing to the freedom, only in accordance with the will of the God.

CHAPTER FIFTEEN

Eternity

Life is infinite, i.e. the endless. Life is a continuous journey. Birth is a beginning for an end. Death is an end for a beginning. A loop has no beginning and end. Time has no end. Eternity is the state or the time after the death. We are souls. Soul is eternal. Eternity is an endless chain of present moments. The present life is a prelude to the eternity. Love creates eternity. Mind relates the eternity with the time. Love is space and time. God has given eternal life to all of us without exception. End is not the destiny of any being or any entity in this existence. We are "the eternal beings". Eternity is forever, so is the love. Eternity is going on through all times. Place is the space, and time is the eternity. Only love is permanent, i.e. the unconditional love. Time creates the eternity, and eternity creates the time. The concept of time is the creation of mind, so as to deal with the memories. Nature explains the time through the changes and the varied experiences, through the events happening in the surroundings and the environment. God is eternal. Life is eternal. All the dimensions of this existence or the creation including the time and the space are eternal, with no beginning and end. Limitations are created by the inabilities of being's sense-perception. In this creation, everything is bounteous, eternal and boundless. Matter and energy both are eternal. Brain of a normal being cannot understand and experience the eternity. True eternity can only be comprehended by the enlightened beings. Do meditation to experience the eternity. Happiness is an inner experience, an inner journey. All the happiness is inside only. There are five koshas (bodies) or sheaths or layers, inside the beings. The fives sheaths from the outmost sheath to the innermost sheath are Annamaya Kosha or the Food Sheath or the Physical Body, Pranamaya Kosha or the Vital Sheath or the Energy Body, Manomaya Kosha or the Mental Sheath or the Mental Body, Vijnanamaya Kosha or the Intellectual Sheath or the Wisdom Body, and Anandamaya Kosha or the Bliss Sheath or the Bliss Body. Starting from the outermost kosha or sheath or layer or body, and moving to the core of the self, each kosha or sheath or layer or body is made up of increasingly subtler degrees of energy. These five koshas or sheaths or layers or bodies exist together, and are encased or nested within one another. Physical Body is the outermost layer, while the innermost layer contains the bliss body or the soul. Once Bliss Body is experienced, real eternal happiness is reached. The Quantum Physics also recognizes that human subtle anatomy as composed of five energy layers or envelopes, viz. the Physical, the Vital, the Mental, the Supramental, and the Bliss. Happiness is an inner journey of experiencing, starting from the Physical Body, and moving towards the Bliss Body. Bliss is the perfect happiness i.e. the eternal happiness. When the "life-infinity" meets the "happiness-eternity", the purpose of life is fulfilled. It is the highest stage of being's overall growth and development in all aspects, viz. physical, religious, and the spiritual. In this state and the stage of development, beings can use the forces and powers of the universe. The universe opens its secret doors. Happiness-eternity, though quite rare, is a sheer blessing in the life, a state of divinity, when the God befriends you.

CHAPTER SIXTEEN

Well-being

Being well is being happy. If one is happy, then only, he or she is well. Well-being is joyfulness. Wellness is internal, and also, external. Well-being depends on managing the surroundings and the self. The only beings, which truly deserve to be in one's life, are those, which treat him or her with love, care, kindness and respect. Choice of beings is important for one's well-being. Well-being is a state of being healthy and happy. Health is the "state of being". Health refers to physical, mental, and social well-being. Wellness aims at enhancing the well-being. Wellness is the state of being healthy, a state of good mental, physical and emotional health. Wellness is the act of practising healthy habits so that instead of just surviving, one is thriving. Dimensions of wellness are spiritual wellness, mental wellness, emotional wellness, physical wellness, social wellness, financial wellness, environmental wellness and the vocational wellness. These dimensions are interdependent, and also, greatly influence each other. If anyone dimension of well-being is out of balance, other dimensions are adversely affected. Make self a priority. Mind of the being creates well-being or miseries. Manage the mind. Health is wealth. Do not live in the past, as it makes a being sad. Also, do not live in the future, as it makes a being anxious. Just, live in the present moment, and be peaceful. Every cell of the body must be healthy. Do meditation. Do Yoga. Play sports. Think, talk and act positive. Be positive. Be the master of your life. Well-being is a journey, a journey replete with commitment, hope, faith and belief. Well-being brings the happiness. Well-being is improved by connecting with other beings. Have good relations and the relationships. Be physically active. Learn new skills. Be a giver. Be a doer. Pay attention to the present moment, as it is the mindfulness. Spend quality time with friends, the loved ones and the beings you trust. Talk about, and express the feelings. Eat well. Challenge and set to test, self-capability. Relax, and enjoy hobbies. Set realistic goals. Walk in the nature. Talk to the nature. Look up at the heavens. Open-up the arms and stretch, as if you are holding the space. Pray to the God. Experience the God. Empower the self. We are the gods. Learn the skills of communication with the universe. The God is inside all the beings. Undertake the inner journey. Talk less. Eat less. Drink more water. Be enthusiastic. Health is enthusiasm. Well-being is fundamental to the health, and also, to the happiness. The secret of a happy life is to live joyfully and peacefully in a state of good overall health.

CHAPTER SEVENTEEN

Divinity

No being is born happy, but, every being has innate ability to create the happiness in his or her life. Always be proud of yourself, for your hard works, for the efforts made, and for how hard you are trying. Life is replete with tests and challenges. Problems are the part of the life. Do not fear anything. Have courage to face these odds, and on the other side of it, success, satisfaction and the eternal happiness are waiting. Every smile, every loving word which is spoken, and every kind action which is performed, is a reflection of the beauty of the soul. Divinity is the state or quality of being divine. Meditation helps in listening to the divine within. Meditation nourishes and blossoms the divinity within. Be humane. Nobility, i.e. the quality of being noble in character, is the guardian divinity. Every soul is divine. Divinity is spread all over, see it and experience it. Faith rests on divine love. Every being is divinity in disguise. Realise it, and manifest it, and then, one finds that everything is harmoniously arranged around him or her. Divinity is realisation of the self. Healing is an experience of the divinity within. Self is the whole creation, source, and also, the end, of everything. Become neutral to reception, reactions and the responses. Divinity is experiential in nature, and expressed through behaviour.

Reduce personal needs and desires. Embrace every being, and everything, as it is, when it comes, during the journey of the life. Inclusivity is divinity. I am another you. Inclusivity and identifying the self with others and other things brings eternal peace and happiness. Spirit expands. Happiness is an experience, an inner experience. Undertake inner journey. Everything is in divinity, and divinity is in everything. Nature is divinity. Divinity radiates peace. It brings sheer joy. It increases one's real beauty. State of bliss is attained through the experience of divinity. Divinity is experienced, when the life unfolds and expresses itself in newer ways by overcoming its limitations. Worshipping invokes the divinity within. Meditation creates awareness of divinity. Realisation of divinity within is called enlightenment. Being divinity is the state of Nirvana. Nirvana is a transcendent state. In this state of transcendence, there are no sufferings, desires, and the sense of self. Nirvana is the final goal. In Nirvana, a being is released from effects of karma, and the cycle of death and rebirth. Unity with the God is divinity. Expression of love awakens the divinity within. Humanity is divinity. Life is a spark of divinity. Become pure, and find the portals of divinity everywhere in the surroundings. Universe has its hidden doors. It is the biggest secret. Connect with the spirit. Every being is the divine flame. Divinity is the supreme state of happiness, i.e. the bliss. Divinity is boundless, beyond the time and the space, and all dimensions. Divinity is infinity. Experience the infinity in order to access the divinity, i.e. the profundity of life. Live an exuberant life.

CHAPTER EIGHTEEN

Smile

Always carry a contagious, and a toxic smile. A smile increases the face value of beings. Never do away with the smile due to the problems of the life. Problems are the part of the life. Problems come in the life, to identify, to realise the true hidden potential, and then, to rise above all. Love the life. Live the life like a phoenix. Phoenix after burning itself on a funeral pyre rises from its own ashes, with a much renewed youth to live through yet another cycle of life. Why to fret about the challenges, problems, encumbrances, difficulties and circumstance of the life? Why to keep crying the same problem time and again? Why to hold on to it? It had come, let it go now. Life is an attitude; develop the right attitude to live it. Beings do not know how to live the life. We die and take birth, several times a day. Anxiety kills the every moment of life. Being alive is being exuberant. A loss of enthusiasm and the happiness is the death. In the state of worry, fulfilment cannot be experienced. Challenges, difficulties and troubles are the part of God's made plan of the life for each one of us here. The plan of the life is always amazing, no matter what it is or what is going on. Life cannot be comprehended by the normal beings, except the few enlightened ones. A self-realised or enlightened being understands the design of the life. God is the player of the life, and we are the spectators of life. Live the life as a spectator. Witness the events of life without drawing any conclusion or making judgement. Nothing is for real here. All is an illusion. Life is a big illusion. Life is a drama. Everything is constantly changing here in this mysterious and intriguing infinite creation. Why, how and when of the life are known, only to the nature, or to the universe and to the God. Learn to smile in the midst of the problems, challenges and crises. The material world, where we all live, is ever changing. Neither the bad, nor the good, is going to stay here, but soon it is going to change. There is not even a single reason to be serious about the life, just be sincere towards the life. Keep smiling. Smile is like the electricity, and the life is like a battery. Whenever we smile, battery of the life gets charged, and a beautiful life journey is initiated, and also, gets activated for getting the happiness. Smile is the spark of the life. Smile must be addictive. If you confront someone without a smile, give him or her, one of yours. A smile is a curve, having the ability to set, the things straight, in the life. Smile reduces the distance between two beings. Smile is an expression of love. In this existence, only love is real and permanent. Smile is the expression of the soul, and the beauty of the soul. Love is the characteristic of the soul. Smile is the real beauty. Smile is a therapy in itself. Smile increases the face value. Smile must be full of affection and warmth. Smile is a sign language, a language of approachability, a language of kindness. Smile brings joy and pleasure. Smile brings peace. Smile makes a being to see the miracles happening in the life. Smile has the power to change the world. When everything fails, smile works. Smile makes the life beautiful. Smile makes one to see the good side of everything. Smile is the wealth of life. Every being is responsible for his or her happiness. Take a decision to become happy, and to remain happy. Do not give the control of happiness to other being, but keep it with yourself. Take charge of your happiness, as it is your wealth. Smile is a gift. Be a pleasant being. Life does not happen one's ways. Life has its own ways. Stop wasting the time, and work on the self. Hammer the unpleasantness, and create and retain the pleasantness. The world, all the experiences of the life, all the expressions of the life, and the life itself, are within. External is essentially internal, and the internal is always controllable. What is external may not be controllable, but there is nothing external, as all is internal. Happiness, joy, peace, bliss, ecstasy, satisfaction, sweetness, or even their opposites, all are internal. Pleasantness and unpleasantness, both are being's internal creations. Work on the inner, and keep what is wished for, and eliminate and annihilate, what is unwanted and not wished. Meditation, Yoga, spiritual practises, religious practises helps in inner development and improvement. Have control on the mind, which in turn, will create control on the thoughts, and thoughts are everything. Everything is created from the thoughts. All the actions good or bad are generated from the thoughts. Be consciously silent. Silence is never silent. It is very powerful. Stop all the agitations, the silence will begin to grow inside. See the silence of Buddha. In silence, lie peace and harmony, joy and happiness, prosperity and wealth, and the success. Smile is created in the state of silence. Smile, as it is the source of instant happiness.

CHAPTER NINETEEN

Love

Love is time-less and space-less. Love transcends all the dimensions of the existence. Love is perpetual. Love is for all times. Love is eternal. Only love is real and permanent. Life runs on love. Love is speechless. Love is the God. Love is the best experience of the life. Love is special. There is nothing as powerful as the love. Love is priceless. Love yourself first. Love the God. Love the nature. Discover your qualities, as it helps appreciation of self. Similarly, discover the qualities of other beings, in order to appreciate them. Discovery of qualities gives rise to the love. Discovery of qualities creates the importance of self, and of others, in one's life. Discovery of the qualities in the other being(s), creates a cooperative and harmonious relationship, and companionship, and eventually brings the happiness in the life. Similarly, closeness or the nearness, and the love, to / for the God, are based on the discovery of attributes related to the God. These attributes of the God are powers, mercy and the compassion, which are very easily evident in the surroundings, and also, in the journey of the life. God is the creator of everything, and this aspect, builds the strongest relationship of one's love with the God. The God created everything from nothingness. God is the reason for existence of all. We have been fashioned into this existence by the God. God creates our worlds to live. The world has been created to be favourable and propitious. Everything in the existence is such that it helps us to unfold our real potential, and then allows us to grow. Even in every failure, there is a great learning, and many other hidden positive aspects. Everything in the life is the design created by the God, the best design, which is for good only. Success is not our achievement, and not created by us, but there is a direct hand of the God in it. Life runs at the mercy of the God. Submit yourself completely before the God, in order to become happy in the life. Prostrate or bow down before the God. Discovery of the creator leads to the discovery of humility within. This humility leads to the discovery of the God and the discovery of peace, satisfaction and the happiness. Happiness is the goal and the very purpose of life. Happiness comes, when soul evolves, and the self-growth takes place. Power is needed for harming others and inflicting pains, whereas, to achieve everything in the life, only love is adequate. Give time to everything, in order to see its real face. Even to the time, give the time. Everything in this life and in this creation just happens at its most suitable time. Birth does not occur before birth. Death does not occur before death. Everything is well time and space coordinated. Life is woven with the threads of dimensions. Time and space are two important dimensions of the life. Manifest plainness, embrace simplicity, reduce selfishness, and have few desires, as it is the mantra of the happiness in the life. Listen with curiosity, speak with honesty, and act with full integrity. The secret of happiness is freedom, and the secret of freedom is courage. Always be grateful, i.e. grateful to every other thing. In the life, every sunrise must hold the promises, and every sunset must hold the peace. Express your gratitude and be thankful to others, and to, every other thing, which is the part of the life. Keep smiling, and, do not hurt other(s), as these are the simpler ways to the happiness, i.e. the secrets of happiness. To be, or not to be, is always one's choice. To love or not to love, is a choice. To be happy or not to be happy is a choice. Life always gives many options. Consciously choose the right one. But remember, what we give, the same is being returned, and this is how, the universe works. Give love in order to get loved. Love everything. We are everything, and everything is us. Being returns the way, the way he or she comes into the life. We always gain by giving love, and never lose. Love is a beautiful conspiracy of the universe. Where there is love, there is life. Be in love with the every moment of the life. Love the life, in turn, the life will love you. Love is a very powerful force. Other's love creates the strength, whereas; love for others creates the courage. Real love awakens the soul. Love given, is the love kept. It is the strength and the power of love, which wins the hearts, and creates a caring and loving world. Fall in love with the whole universe. Real love, is felt, seen and shown. Love converts "I" into "we" or "us". Love the self, first. Love is the language of the soul. Love is the expression of the soul. Love is the characteristic of the soul. The happiness, which is felt, is in direct relationship with the love, which is given, and received.

CHAPTER TWENTY

Hope

Hope is the only thing, which is stronger than the fear. Hope is the power, which gives a being, the confidence to step out, and to try. Hope is the life. Life and death are not different. Life is the strength. Death is the weakness. Strength is the weakness. And, weakness is the strength. Hope is the feeling of wanting something to happen, and thinking that it will. Hope is cherishing a desire in anticipation. Hope reduces the feeling of helplessness. Hope increases happiness. Hope reduces stress. Hope improves quality of life. When the struggles of the life and the storms toss the being(s), hope acts as an anchor. Hope is the anchor for the soul, quite firm and secure. Hope arises, when one has connections with good and positive beings, and the higher power. Hope is stimulated by, breathing, meditation, prayer, spirit contact, impermanence, sleep, quietness, and witnessing or experiencing the acts of love, goodness, and the kindness. Lack of hope causes depression and anxiety. Hope increases the sense of meaning in life. Hope helps in identification and realization of goals of the life. Hope keeps the dreams alive. In the midst of adversities, hope becomes the saviour. Keep high hopes. Set loftier goals. Hope helps in realisation of these goals. Hope is the predictor of success. Hope is, believing good things will happen, while keeping unshakeable and undeterred faith in the higher power. Hope helps one to look only on the brighter side of the things. Hope converts the challenges into the opportunities. Hope is the confident expectation of righteousness. Hope is the longing for the promised blessings of righteousness. Hope is a gift. Hope is nurtured by positive thinking, staying upbeat, focusing on the positive, practising the forgiveness, helping the others, seeking the inspiration, and engaging in the religious and the spiritual works and practices. Hope is inspired by demonstrating love and care, acceptance, appreciation, staying connected and helping the others to find their passion. Hope is a power. Hope makes one to see the light in the extreme darkness. Hope is necessary for the life. Anything becomes possible by hope. Hope is a waking dream. Hope is the best medicine. Hope helps in dreaming and imagining. Without the rain, there is no rainbow. Therefore, face the struggles of the life, while using the power of hope. Future is a hope. Success is a hope. It is the hope, which makes one to attempt the impossible, and make it possible. Hope holds the soul. Keep infinite hope. Hope is the last attempt in every precarious situation of the life. Never feel like giving up or leaving or ending. Learn patience and perseverance, and develop the ability to hold on to the things, even if not good at the moment. It is the power of hope, which makes the ugly beautiful. Give time, its needed time. Hold on. Life does not throw any challenge, which cannot be handled. Nature knows strengths and weaknesses of every being. Life is not same for all. Life is designed differently for different beings by the God, in such a way, that it could be handled by them. Life is a test, and the purpose of tests is, to make the being(s), to evolve, to grow, to become big, to get strong, to become responsible, to become wise, to develop a right thinking, to get enlightened, to do the right actions, for the happiness. Challenges and the struggles of the life, help a being, in deepening his or her roots. Do not compare self with the others. All are different. Our karmas are different. Our destinies are different. Our life journeys are different. Our personalities are different. Our happiness is different. Our sorrows are different. Yet, hope is common to all, accessible and available to all. Hope is always there, to help us, to sail through the choppy waters of the life, so as to reach the other side safely, where success and the happiness are waiting. We serve different purposes in this creation. Relax, be patient, but keep working. Things happen at the right time. No hurry, no worry, no early, and no late. Happiness is the craziest equation of the mathematics of the life, as it multiplies, when being divided. Every little thing matters in the life, in order to do or to achieve the big in the life. Gold is found in the dirt. In the midst of the darkness, while riding the horse of the hope, and galloping in the pursuit of light, success is met, and the treasure of happiness is found.

CHAPTER TWENTY-ONE

Silence

Silence is never silent. Develop the ability to listen the sound of silence. Silence is very powerful, as silence is power in itself. Silence is the source of great strength. Silence means "Nishabd", which means to have no words. Silence is not doing, but becoming. When words fail, silence takes over, and speaks. Silence is being's true friend in all times and spaces. Silence is the hardest argument. It is the silence, which brings forth the truth. Silence retains one's dignity. Silence means adaptation. Silence creates self-healing. As one gets smarter, he or she speaks less and understands more. We are energy-beings. Silence conserves the energies of the beings. Silence is expressive. Silence expresses pains and pleasures both. Pain is not always in tears, but most often, it is also present in the smile. Silence is the smile of the soul. If speech is a river, then silence is an ocean. Yoga and meditation bring the state of silence. It is the silence, when one is able to connect to him or her true self. Inner journey happens in the silence. In the state of silence only, one can listen the sounds of the universe, and can establish communication with the universe. "AUM" is theard in the silence. It is the force and the power of life and the existence. Work hard and harder in the silence, and let, the success make the noise. Silence has answers to all the questions. Silence is never empty. Silence is a therapy, rather one of the best therapies. The God is experienced in the silence. Silence is the art of conversation. Silence is a beautifully uttered nice poem, which is full of peace. Silence is the secret of happiness. Patience and the silence both are very strong energies. Patience brings mental strength, whereas, silence brings the emotional strength. Silence is wisdom's best reply in all extreme situations. Silence nourishes the wisdom. Silence is louder than the loudest word(s). Silence establishes the strongest connection with the environment, nature and the existence. Silence is an experience of the creation and the creator, and the beyond. Silence does not need explanations. Those beings, which cannot understand one's silence, can also, never understand his or her spoken words. Soul speaks in the silence. At the end, being and his or her real or true self only remains. Self is the silence. Silence is the life. Mind is conquered in the state of silence. Birth is silence. Death is a deep silence. Beautify the self, with the silence. Silence is the best reply. Speak, only when, words are better than the silence. Silence is music. Silence increases are levels of awareness and concentration. Silence enhances or improves the consciousness. Silence is the journey from the compulsiveness to the consciousness. Nature has silent-sound. Silence is the peace. Wind has its own silent-sound. Water has its own silent-sound. Fire has its own silent-sound. Space is filled with silent-sound. Silence is joyfulness and the happiness. Silence is the answer to all the questions and the confusions of / in the life. Silence unknots the knots of the life, and knots the things, which should be. Gods are always in the state of silence. Silence is beautiful. Silence is not the denial of articulation, on the contrary, it is the best and the strongest articulation. Silence is the song. Silence is the dance. Silence is the loudest scream. Silence is the speech. At the core of anything and everything, there is silence, whereas, at the surface, there is always some sound. Sound is created due to restraints, resistance and restrictions, and when these are beings removed, sound turns into the silence. Silence is the freedom, i.e. the freedom of the life, as experienced by the soul. Silence heals the wounds, and takes away all the pains of toil. Silence is beyond all dimensions. Silence expands being's aura. Silence is the grace of life.

CHAPTER TWENTY-TWO

Health

Physical health, mental health and the emotional health, affect the life of every being. To remain healthy in the life, one must regularly take certain physical diet, religious diet and the spiritual diet. Yoga, meditation and sports maintain a good overall health of a being. One grows old, when he or she stops being creative, and therefore, one can become old at any age and stage of the life. Ability to heal is the health. Health is a state of complete physical, mental, and social well-being. Five aspects of health are physical, emotional, social, spiritual, and the intellectual. Health brings wellness. Health is wealth. Wellness has seven dimensions, viz. physical, mental, spiritual, social, financial, environmental, and the vocational. Physical body is the house of soul or the spirit. This physical body or the gross body houses all other bodies. Kundalini is the energy, which is coiled at the base of the spine like a serpent. Kundalini is the dormant energy inside the body. Kundalini Yoga is the system of meditation, which is directed towards the release of the Kundalini Energy. Kundalini Shakti or Kundalini Power arises, when it passes through seven energy Chakra or seven subtle-energy centres, inside the body. When Kundalini Energy flows freely upwards through the seven Chakra, then it leads to an expanded state of the Consciousness, and this process is known as "Kundalini Awakening". There are seven Chakra, which are related to the seven bodies. Awaken the Chakra for good health and happiness, and the expanded consciousness. These Chakra are the Root Chakra, the Sacral Chakra, the Solar Plexus Chakra, the Heart Chakra, the Throat Chakra, the Third Eye Chakra, and the Crown Chakra. Seven bodies have their seven corresponding Chakra, one for each. At the first level, there are three bodies, viz. the Physical Body, the Astral Body and the Causal Body. Body is also termed as the Kosha. Physical Body is also called as the Bhautik Sharira, and it corresponds to the Annamay Kosha, or the Gross Body. Astral Body is the Subtle Body, also known as Sukshma Sharir. The Astral Body corresponds to the the Pranamaya Kosha, the Manomaya Kosha, and the Vigyanmaya Kosha. The Causal Body is also called as the Karan Sharir. Causal Body corresponds to the Anandamaya Kosha. At the second level, there are five bodies. These are the Gross Body or the Annamaya Kosha, the Life Force Body or the Pranamaya Kosha, the Mind Body or the Manomaya Kosha, the Intellect or the Special Knowledge Body or the Vigyanamaya Kosha, and the Bliss Body or the Anandmaya Kosha. The Physical Body is made up of gross material; therefore, it is also called as Gross Body (Sthool Sharira or the Annamaya Kosha). The Astral Body is subtler than the Physical Body. Astral Body exists within the Physical Body. Astral Body has much higher level of awareness than the Physical Body. Presence of the Astral Body can be felt, while standing very close to someone. The Casual Body exists within the Astral Body. The Causal Body is even more subtle than the Astral Body. The Causal Body is the being's seed state. The Causal Body moves from one birth to the next. For good health, and the happiness, it is necessary to purge and purify all the bodies. When bodies are purified, then a being becomes harmonious or Sama. Sama means equal or even. In the state of good health, soul becomes beautiful. In the state of good health, pleasant fragrance or smell is emitted or exuded, and also, the voice becomes resonant. Appetite increases in the state of good health. In the state of good health, one becomes full-hearted, energetic, and quite strong. The physical body becomes lean and bright. If the Nadi System is pure, state of good health is achieved. Nadi means channel or pathway or nerve. Nadi is the channel of Prana or the life force or the life energy, inside the body. In the human body, there are 72,000 Nadi. These 72,000 Nadi spring from another three basic Nadi. There is a Left Nadi, a Right Nadi and a Central Nadi. These are known as Ida, Pingala, and Sushumna, respectively. At the higher level for enlightened beings, there is an experience of total seven bodies. These seven bodies are the Physical Body or the Bhautik Sharira or the Annamaya Kosha, the Etheric Body or the Sukshma Kosha or the Pranamaya Kosha, the Astral Body or the Ling Sharira, the Mental Body or the Manomay Sharira, the Spiritual Body or the Adhyatmik Sharira or Vigyanmay Kosha, the Cosmic Body or the Bhrahmm Sharira or the Anandmaya Kosha, and the Empty Body or the Nirvanic Sharira or the Shunya Sharir. Mooladhara or Root Chakra is associated with the Physical Body. Swadhisthana or the Sacral Chakra is blocked by the fear, especially the fear of death. Opening this chakra boosts creativity and the confidence. Sacral Chakra is associated with the Etheric Body. Manipura or the Solar Plexus Chakra is associated with Astral Body. Anahata or the Heart Chakra is associated with Mental Body. Vishuddhi or the Throat Chakra is associated with the Spiritual Body. Agya or the

Third Eye Chakra is associated with the Cosmic Body. And, Sahastrara or the Crown Chakra is associated with the Empty Body. Do Meditation and Yoga for good health, and the happiness, in the life, as health is the happiness. Cleanse and detox the body on a regular basis. The God gives us two gifts each day. One is the Choice, and the other is the Chance. Choice is for a good life, and the Chance is for making the life, "the best". At the end, you have only yourself. Beings are not loved because of their money or the position or the power or the skills, but for their values, their compassion and their love for the others. Giving and receiving the pure love, is the sign of good health, and brings the real eternal happiness in the life.

CHAPTER TWENTY-THREE

Positivity

Always, be positive. Melt away all negativity. Positivity is power. It is a force in itself. Positivity uplifts and empowers the being(s). Keep spreading positivity, wherever you go. Things, waited and hoped for, tend to arrive at the most unexpected and appropriate moments, and numerous inexplicable ways, in the journey of the life. Be full of love, compassion and mercy. Hearts can only be won by being kind and considerate, and by love. Positivity is happiness. Being positive, is getting spiritually empowered. Sharing is caring, and this thought, and the action therefrom, is quite positive, and brings immense happiness. Try touching the lives of others, and there are many good and positive ways of doing it. It is the real happiness of the life. Inhale blessings and exhale gratitude. In the end, you have only yourself. Always keep hoping for the good in the life. Keep a green tree in the heart, and the singing birds will come automatically. Be like a tree, staying grounded, connected strongly with the roots, and bending before breaking. Enjoy the inner beauty, the true self. Keep growing. Positivity is the practice of being positive or optimistic in the attitude. When one is positive, he or she engages him or herself in the positive thinking, which in turn generates positive emotions, leading to positive behaviour like the acts of kindness and the generosity. Positivity is maintaining calmness, composure and the hopefulness. Positivity is enthusiasm. Positivity is the energy and the love for the life. When one is positive, he or she perceives things differently, which further enables him or her to feel more positive. Thus, positivity brings more positivity. It proliferates. Positive beings have greater work productivity. Also, such beings engage in greater emotional self-regulation and self-control. Positivity is quite gratifying in its nature, and the gratification brings sheer happiness in the life. Positive beings are sociable and have stronger networks. Positive thinking is very powerful. The simpler ways of being or staying positive are doing Yoga, Meditation, playing sports, working on hobbies, using affirmations, focussing on the present moment, reminding the self to focus on the good things only no matter how small they are, surrounding self with other positive beings, and doing nice to others. Positivity is contagious, and also infectious. Positivity develops positive attitude. Positive attitude means being optimistic about the situations, interactions, and the self. Positive attitude keeps one always hopeful and makes him or her to see "the best" in every situation. Staying positive brings a big change in the life, and creates a big difference. Train the mind. Positivity is a choice. Happiness depends upon quality of thoughts. Happiness is a mood. Only a happy being can make others happy. Struggles in the life develop strength(s) in the life. Life is a big struggle for all. Positivity is a mindset. Don't be afraid of, to change, or to grow. Be open to all kinds of criticism, and learn, and change if needed. Learn, unlearn and re-learn, as it is the mantra of success and the happiness in the life. Work on the relations and the relationships. Beings come in the life with certain purpose.

Hobnob with the great, and the good. Positivity always wins. Positive mind creates positive vibes, which in turn, makes the life positive. Trust the timings of the acts and the events in the life. Do not complain. Good things only happen, when one is positive, it is how the nature and the universe operate. A positive being sees the opportunities in every challenging and demanding situation or circumstance and the hardship. A positive being sees the invisible, feels the intangible, and makes the impossible, possible. In dire straits, just look up, talk to the heavens, and then, you find help rushing to you, and the solace descending. Always remember the God. Keep his name on the tongue. Make the God, your all-time best friend. Make the God the constant companion of the life, and then live free. Then, the happiness is all yours, and the problems are of the life companion, i.e. the God. Life is too short, but very beautiful. Tough times do not last for long. Do good, and the good only, will be returned. Focus on yourself, and not on the others. Remove negative thoughts. Remove the negative energy. Raise the vibrations at home and at the workplace. Do not fear anything. Manage yourself well. Manage the body, thoughts, emotions, and the energies. Life is openness. Life is exploring everything. Life is living free, and enjoying the infinite freedom. We all are born free to live free, and complete the journey of the life in full freedom. Life is for growth and the evolution. Stay motivated. Live an effusive live in extreme profusion. What one can think of, is already there in the nature, take from the nature. Nature is just, equitable and generous. "Being human" is a tremendous possibility, therefore, do all, which is good, if possible. Challenge yourself. Beings can become gods. There are no limitations in the life, and in this vast creation. Limitations are the false creations of the mind.

The creator of this creation is limitless. God is infinite. Every being is also infinite in essence. The life is limitless and infinite. Life is a continuum. Life is a continuous journey. A thought can do everything. One positive thought and one positive action of each being are good enough to fill the life all over the globe, with immense positivity. Finally, live happily.

CHAPTER TWENTY-FOUR

Good Habits

Never go to the bed without a dream, and try waking up without any purpose. Beings must be poetry in motion, in their all interactions, and the behaviour. Have the right attitude. One does not need to be perfect to inspire the others, but, simply needs to be honest. The best and most precious gift, which can be given to any being, is our attention. Keep spreading positivity, wherever you go. Right attitude and a strong commitment bring excellence. Beings, who bathe with water, change their dress, but the beings who bathe themselves with their sweat, write the history. Good habits are repetitive actions or the behaviour, which one wishes to repeat. Good habits have positive physical, emotional, and psychological consequences. On the contrary, bad habits are those actions, which if repeated, will have negative consequences. Interestingly, some bad habits are harmless. But, many other bad habits are quite harmful, and also, have a much deeper, long-term impact. Good habits, when worked upon, create a good or positive energy. Bad habits, when worked upon, create a bad or negative energy. The acts of good or positive energies are giving, being creative, forgiving, kindness, trust, being diligent, maintaining calmness, being proactive, honesty, selflessness, love, being loyal, staying motivated, being joyful, being efficient, getting inspired, expressing gratitude, bravery, being happy and being passionate. Acts of bad or negative energy are making complaints, inferiority, being selfish, being impatient, being dishonest, being fearful, sadness, anger, being lazy, getting violent, jealousy, being ignorant, getting confused, greed, hate, arrogance, procrastination, becoming self-centred, being fake, hypocrisy, ego, regrets, being superficial, hopelessness, stress and getting worried. Good habits lead to happiness in the life. Goodness leads to the godliness. Good habits are continually practised positive behaviour. Good habits are exercising, eating healthy, reading, spending quality time with family, good sleep, being courteous to everyone, being responsible and practising meditation. Morality, integrity and honesty are best habits. Good habit is the quality of abiding by strong moral principles. Being's habit(s) determine his or her future. Life is changed only by changing something, which is done on a daily basis. The secret of success and the happiness is found in the daily routine. Motivation makes the start, and the habit, keeps it going. Habits are addictive in their nature. Bad habits are counteracted and controlled only by the Good habits. Every being must learn to, create, learn, love and move. Habit is the lack of awareness. It is good to follow the "good" unawares, than following the "bad". Good habits lead to good life. We become what we repeatedly do. The "excellence" should not be an act, but should be a habit. Habits make us. Good habits make us good. Bad habits make us bad. Getting little better each day, counts a lot, for the life. Don't be preoccupied, than being busy. Handle the emotions and the thoughts properly and efficiently. Wake up early in the morning. Do not fear the failure. Fail fast, so as to rise again quickly. Life is a living possibility; anything is possible, just think for it and act on it. Life is the good hap design by the God. Success is earned. Happiness is created. No other being creates other's happiness. Happiness is self-creation. Take charge of the time. Time and energy when combined, determine the life. Manage the mind. Master the energies. Experience the universe. Don't struggle within. Do physical exercises. Apply creativity, and try creating something new. Newness brings freshness. Learn to live alone. Explore the self. Divinity is within each one of us. All the experiences of life are within. Life is within, i.e. inside, and not the outside. Universe is within. God is within. Inside is the outside. Internal is the external. Thoughts are inside. Actions are internally created. Habits are internal, but manifested externally. And, the happiness is also internal. Life needs to be engineered. Inner journey needs to be undertaken. One's internal, decides his or her, quality of life.

CHAPTER TWENTY-FIVE

Habit Of Giving

By giving, we earn more. By giving, no being has ever become poor. Giving is an expression of love. Do not just make a living, but make the life. Living is made by getting, but the life is made by giving. What is given, always comes back, in a much bigger way, direct or indirect. Give to inspire the others. Put full love in giving. Follow the habit of giving passionately. Always, be generous, be kind, and be merciful and loving. Sharing is caring. Words inspire, thoughts provoke, but it is the action, which brings a being closer to his or her dreams in the journey of life. It is our belief system in the life, which makes us, what we are. Believe and feel, what you want to become, and you will become. It is no magic, but a simple rule, and one of the laws of the nature. Belief changes the attitude. And the change in attitude brings changes in the action(s). What we think, we become. Right attitude is necessary to live the life in its essence. Live the life in profusion and exuberance. Good life and its happiness, is all about the right attitude in the life. Work on your thought process, if not right. And then, act, and keep patience. Give time to time. Rights things happen at the right time. Right things will happen in the life. Universe helps. God is definitely there. One and the supreme, prevailing energy of this vast existence is "the God". God is energy. Consciousness is energy. We are also energy. Soul or the spirit, is the energy, which is only real we. Body is matter or the material. Matter or the material is not eternal, but the energy is. We all are eternal energy beings. All the time, and at everywhere, there are so many helping spirits, which keep surrounding us, and they help and support us without saying. Yet, one's choices, thoughts and the actions should always be in the right direction in the life. Be honest. Be ethical. Follow morals. Help others. Think and act, as per the instructions from the soul. Soul is always right. Soul is the element of the God, in each one of us. Be good in the eyes of self. Thing, which is not worth saying, is also, not worth doing. Acts of kindness never go in waste. Happiest beings are those, which give more, and not those, which get more. The joy of giving is just unparalleled to any other joy in the life, and one of the biggest joys of the life. In the life, above the need, God gives the things to us, to share and give, and not to hold. Things will stop coming in the life, if not given. It is a secret. Things in profusion and the affluence are given in by the nature, the universe, and the God, to few chosen beings. The acts of giving create a flow of positive energy. Receiving process starts only after the giving process. More is given, more is being received. Demanding has never made any being happy. There is a definite, "Law of Giving", which simply states that, "give joy to get joy", "offer love to get loved", and "help the others to become rich". Giving is a privilege, and not a duty. Learn to give, and not to give up. Things create things. Nature and the universe, also operate according to the Theory of Multiplication. It is known as Proliferation. Joy creates the joy. Happiness creates the happiness. The secret of life, and the life's happiness, lies in the habit of giving.

Sharing Is Caring

Sharing with others brings great satisfaction, joy and the happiness. Share time, and happiness, and fulfil the wishes. "Sharing is caring" is the characteristics of the nature, the universe, the soul and the God. "Sharing is caring", teaches compassion and love. Love is the basis of whole creation and the vast existence. Love is the basis of the life, i.e. pure unconditional love. Caring is loving. And, loving is the life. Thus, the life is all about sharing. Pass on, whatever you have, as we have only that, what somebody had given to us. If nobody gives, then the nature gives, and the God gives. Do the small things of the life with great love. Sharing is caring, is not just an act, but a profound feeling, and makes the lots of good karma to go around. We all live our life through the others. What one gets, make his or her living, but that he or she shares, makes his or her life. My age is not only my age, but also your age. We are always alive in the feelings. Death is the absence of feelings. Feeling is energy, i.e. the vibrations. In the life, we create the experiences, and live the experiences. "Sharing is caring", is a profound experience, create it, and live it. Whatever may be the age, if one is planning for tomorrow, he or she is still young to achieve the planned thing. Dream big, and believe it. Do not die a constipated life. Be mad, i.e. mad at the heart.

Life is a long lesson. Life is a continuous journey. Life is the biggest teacher. The trick lies in, finding out, what the life is trying to teach. Every ending has a new beginning. Never stop putting efforts. Add two more dots to the single dot, as a single dot means, "full stop", but the three dots mean, "and continuing", i.e. an ellipsis. There are simple tips and secrets for a happy life. Look for good in every situation. Laugh more. Ignore other beings, especially if they discourage you. Do not listen to the gossips. Design your own life. Develop an attitude of gratitude. Once it is past, let it go. Be honest. Be straight to the self. God is within all of us. Be an epitome of values. From somebody become nobody, and then, from nobody become everybody. The God is nobody, and yet, everybody. Share the experiences of life. Share the knowledge gained in the life. "Sharing is caring", promotes the understanding. Understanding is love. Apart from sharing and caring, the life is also, smiling, learning, forgiving, laughing, prancing, falling, running, sitting, hugging, wondering, helping, healing, dancing, sleeping, dreaming, playing and even much more. These are the greater experiences of the life, and gifts to each one of us by the God. "Sharing is caring", brings peace and calm, and keeps one tuned with the music of universe, nature and the life. We are here in the life, to learn from each other. Cooperate with others. Shared joy becomes a much increased joy, and shared sorrow becomes a much decreased sorrow. Do acts of kindness. The greatness of a being is to positively affect all those beings, which are around him or her. Be the people's person, and positively impact their lives. "Sharing is caring", is one of the biggest secret of life's happiness.

CHAPTER TWENTY-SEVEN

Killing The Anger

Do not manage the anger, but eliminate it, simply annihilate it, kill it. Suppress the anger, rout it. Control the anger, and also, control the excitement. Anger is the feeling that one has, when something has happened, or somebody has done something, which is not liked. Anger is a strong feeling of displeasure or annoyance or dislike. Anger is unpleasant, unpleasant to the self, and also, unpleasant to the others. Anger is an aggression. Kill the anger, before it kills you. The types of anger are Passive Aggression, Open Aggression, and the Assertive Anger. Anger weakens the soul. It is detrimental to all types of health, viz. physical, mental and the emotional. Refrain from anger. Forsake wrath. Do not fret. Anger leads to the evil, all sorts of evils. Anger spoils the relations, and also, the relationships. Be patient. Right things happen to the right beings at the right time in the journey of life. Nature is never discriminatory. What is "right", will only happen. God has his own plan for each one of us. Nature has its own design. Universe has also thought something for each one of us. Life has its own trajectory. In the state of anger, become silent. Do Yoga and meditation, and then, anger will be controlled in natural way. Work on anathemas. Anger does not solve problems, but simply aggravates them. Peace is the characteristic of the soul, food of the soul. Anger is a gaol, whereas, peace is liberation, freedom. Pain is underneath, every anger. Why pain? There is no reason to be painful in the life in any event, or situation and circumstance. Train the mind, as fear is the trick and a play of the mind, in order to make painful and miserable. Use the power of subconscious mind correctly. Use the power of positive thinking. Truth cannot be found in the state of anger, similar to as one cannot see his or her reflection in the boiling water. Never ever lose the peace of mind. Peace is the biggest treasure of life, and the source of happiness in the life. Be religious. Be spiritual. Be an awakened being. Be a truly educated being, and not just a qualified being. Qualification does not guarantee right education. Right education, teaches the lessons of the life, and analyses the actions and the reactions in the life. Anger is a battle within, to be won, and not to be lost. Do not crumple or crumble under the pain. Develop the capacity to change the self. In many life's situations, peace is better than being right. Love all. Anger simply creates wounds. Peace is a healer. No good work is possible in the state of anger. Good work is only possible, when one is calm, equable, forgiving and also well-balanced. Learn to forgive and forget. Only true rich beings can forgive and forget. Do not create any new karma. Karma is the biggest trap, and the only reason for birth, death and then rebirth. Anger is an acid. Anger is fire. Anger is a punishment in itself, then why to punish the self. Exercise empathy. Patience and empathy are enemies of anger. Anger is poison. Anger elicits anger. Anger arises from fear or panic. Fear is the parent of anger and hate. Haters are always the confused admirers. Fear elicits fear. Anger is the sign to change. Anger leads to the destruction of everything. Life is precious. To kill the anger, take a long walk. Disengage the self from that state of mind. Listen to the music. Play sports. Look up at the heavens. Talk to the God. Drink water. Eat fresh fruits. Take charge of the mind. In the state of anger, mind does not take the instructions. Take the self-faculties in self-control. Anger is a living death. Delay is a remedy to anger. Best fighter is never angry. Anger is abandoning the wisdom. Spend some time alone, when angry. Anger is not an entity. It does not exist in the natural state of life. One "becomes angry", why to become angry, when it is not for any good, instead become peaceful and happy. Anger is not a conscious act. Let the life, not to become compulsive or the accidental. Life is not a chance happening. Being's consciousness should create the situations in being's life. Learn to live blissfully. Make your faith system strong and stronger, stronger faith in the self, and strongest faith in the God, and the happiness simply comes.

CHAPTER TWENTY-EIGHT

Turning Weakness Into Strength

Weakness is a disadvantage or a fault. Weakness is a character trait or a skill, which is negative. Strength is a character trait or a skill, which is positive. Life is rooted in the reality. Smile without any condition, talk without any intention, give without any reason, and care without any expectation, as all this simply makes all the relations and the relationships beautiful, and also, the life beautiful. These are the secrets of happiness in the life. Life is not about pleasing everyone, but it is about, not hurting anyone. In the journey of life, there are three types of being, which are experienced; one, which make the wonders happen, second, which see the wonders happening, and the third, which wonder, what has happened. Choose the one, which kind you wish to be or become. The secret of happiness is the freedom, and the secret of freedom is the courage. One is always at the right place, and at the exact time, and also, in the right situation. Life is an illusion, a big illusion. Space and time rule the show of the life. Life is a game, play it well. Even a very right decision, which is taken, gets wrong, when it is too late. Life is a game of timings. Respect the time, so that time also respects you. Weaknesses of beings are shyness, taking criticism, self-criticism, lack of knowledge, lack of confidence, public speaking, inability to delegate and the lack of confidence. Strengths of beings are knowledge, attributes, skills, and talents. The tests of the life are not for showing the weakness(s), but for showing the strength(s). Learn to convert the weakness into the strength. One of the secret is that weakness of a being is also his or her strength. Strength lies within the weakness. One's weakness is also his or her strength. One's strength is also his or her weakness. Every being should be quite strong physically, intellectually, and spiritually. Strengths are realised, when one comes face-to-face with his or her weaknesses. In the show and the game of the life, no one saves us, but we only save ourselves. Pessimism is weakness, optimism is strength. Optimism is a power. Weaknesses can be turned into the strength with the right mindset. Mindset is the established set of attitudes. Work on the mind. Do Yoga and Meditation. Weakness of the attitude eventually becomes the weakness of the character. It is foolery to consider the silence as the ignorance, calmness as the acceptance, and the tenderness and the kindness as the weaknesses. Weakness can neither be a reason nor an excuse for anything in any situation. For personal growth and happiness in the life, one must appreciate his or her strengths and weaknesses, both. Never be rude, as rudeness is the imitation of strength of a weak being. Continuous efforts and struggles of the life, give strength, and provide growth in the life. Life is indeed very interesting and beautiful, stay patient, and trust the journey of the life. Believe in, "you can", and you will get. Forgive beings for their bad behaviour or mistakes. Always have a smile, no matter what. Do not hurt any other being. Keep good thoughts, as these provide the strength. Life's challenges help in self-discovery. Faith gives strength. Faith also creates a sense of balance in the life, and a perspective in the life. Without rain, there is no rainbow. Adversities are the facts of life. Gem is created by friction. Life is not about waiting for the storms to pass, but all about dancing, prancing and playing in it. It is often the last key, which opens the doors, therefore, in the journey of the life, keep trying, do not hesitate or fear anything. Every being is immortal. The God is within us only. He, who has led you so far, will also guide you further. Trust in the God. Weakness is the death, and strength is the birth, a rebirth every time.

CHAPTER TWENTY-NINE

Good Relationships

Good relationships keep beings happier and healthier. Social connections are really very good for us. Relationship is the essence of the life. Beings that are more closely socially connected to their family, friends and the community are the happiest ones. Such beings, having good relationships, are much more physically healthier, and live longer, as compared to all those, which are not socially well connected. Loneliness kills. Even in the madding crowd, or in a social occasion, or in a family gathering, or in the milieu, one can be lonely. It is not about the number of friends one has, or his or her committed relationships, but it is all about the quality of the closeness with everything, and with every being, which matters, and brings the real joy and the true happiness. Living in conflicts is quite detrimental to the health. There must be element of affection in every relationship. Warm relationships are always too protective, which is very good. Good relationships protect the body, as well as the brain. Beings with good relationships, possess much sharper and longer memories. Replace the screen time with the beings time. Liven up a broken or a bad relationship, by doing something new and good, together. In the family, in order to build better and stronger relationships, go with the members of the family for vacation tours, or long walks, or date nights. The family, which eats together, stays together. Reach out to that being, which you have not spoken for many years. Fill the life with sweet surprises. A good and a happy life are always built on good relationships. Relationships to remain warm and good, need proper nutrition, which requires behavioural vitamins and the supplements, and a right attitude. Attitude is the mindset. Work on the mind. Do the mind management. Use the powers of subconscious mind in the life. Live a conscious life, and not a compulsive life. Good relationships are always based on strong attachments and strong bonding. When there are no confusions and doubts, but an utmost clarity in the relationships, an attachment and a strong bond are automatically created. Misunderstandings may bring weakness(s) in the bond. Relationships should never be temporary, but should be permanent, based on the real unconditional love. True relationships are always spiritual, and are love connections among the souls. Soul-to-soul connection is eternal. Physical connections are temporary. Always add the element of care to the relationships. Care and protection build the confidence in the relationships. Dedication makes the relationships to go a long way. Dedication increases the immunity of the relationships, and brings warmth to it. No being wants to live in the loneliness. Relationships have their direct connections with the minds. We grow in the relationships in the journey of the life. Good growth needs proper and timely nurturing of the relationships. Relationships need care and attention. Relationships, which get neglected, die out. Relationships need constant care and careful maintenance. Maintaining good relationships is a great self-help. Mistakes in the life happen by situation(s) and circumstances, and not by the intention, therefore, try finding the reasons behind the mistake, as it is the only way of valuing your relations and the relationships. In the life, good relationships, happiness, peace of mind and compassion are more important than any physical attainment or achievement. In the life, everything is achieved, only by the thought(s), the quality of thoughts, whether it is the success or the happiness or something else. Be in loving relationship with the God always. God is the parent or parents, the heavenly parent. Always, stay connected to the earthly parents. Love them, take care of them. Respect them. In good relationships, there is sacrifice, giving attitude, no comparison, forgiveness, forgetfulness and no expectations. Soul inside the body, is in a certain relationship with it. Relationship is the connection. Journey of the life, begins with the establishment of such a relationship, and severed with the end of such a relationship between the soul and the body. In the existence, everything is a show of relationship between matter or the material, and the energy. A happy life is based on good relationships with the nature. Love all, all will love you. What is given comes back. No two things in this intriguing creation are separate and distinct, but everything is just a reflection of the other. I am another you. Loving the others is loving the self. Caring about the others is caring the self. Valuing the others is valuing the self. It is how; the good relationships are being created and carried out. Good relationships are the one, among many other life's happiness secrets.

CHAPTER THIRTY

Happiness

Happiness is an emotional state. Happiness is a sense of well-being. Happiness involves feelings of satisfaction and joy, contentment in life and its fulfilment, and no despair. Happiness involves positive emotions. Life's satisfaction, brings happiness. Happiness is the exuberance of life. Life energies are quite high in the state of happiness. It is not about, how much we have, but all about, how much we enjoy, which brings joy and happiness. Happiness is the feeling, which comes, when life is good. Happiness is opposite of sadness. Beings feel happiness, when they are successful, or they feel safe or lucky. Happiness is not about getting all that you want or wish for, but it is all about enjoying, all that you have in the present. Happiness is only present in the present. Do not try getting the happiness from the past of the future. Past is a memory. Future is a possibility. In essence, there is nothing like past or future, rather, past, present and the future is a single point in the time and space, and not the three distinct points. All is present only. Past, present and future are purely notional, and are fictional creations of the mind, the memory and the intellect. Happiness is associated with self-confidence and self-esteem. Happiness means that one is well pleased with him or herself, may be for his or her choices, and

/ or, may be for the kind of being, which he or she is. Happiness comes with a purpose, like someone to love or something to do or simply something to look forward to. Happier beings have better overall health. Happy beings live longer in comparison to their less happy peers. In the state of happiness, brain is, engaged, creative, productive, energetic and resilient. Happy beings are not held hostage by their life situations and circumstances. Happy beings do not seek happiness in other beings or the physical wealth, accomplishments and the possessions. All this is too ephemeral, but the life is ad infinitum. Happiness comes with the spiritual and religious accomplishments. Happiness is the state of equilibrium of soul, inside the body. Sadness is a play of the mind. Therefore, manage the mind, to not create the sadness, but only the happiness. Happiness is the life. Happiness is the experience of the God. In the state of happiness, being is quite close to the nature, the existence and the God. Happiness is one of the few blessings of the life. Secret of happiness lies in using the power to choose, to accept, what is liked, and to reject, what is disliked. Happiness is found in the present, whereas, excitement is always for something yet to come in the future. Live in the present. If present is good, future will definitely be good, as it is the present, which makes the future. Happiness is always internal and not external. All experiences of the life, even of an external object are internal experiences only. Therefore, work on the inner-self. The inner-self is the real self. Do Yoga and meditation. Work on the mind. Happiness should be a subject of choice, and not a chance happening. Happiness is not a place, but a continuous journey in certain direction. Nothing can make one happy, till he or she chooses or decides to be happy. In the journey of the life, do not wait for the destination to become happy, but try to be happy while on the journey. Do not postpone the happiness. Happiness is the treasure of life, and every being cannot find it. Do not postpone the satisfaction due to the challenges of the life. Happiness is not a destination, but a journey, a journey which must go along with the journey of the life. Manifest plainness, embrace simplicity, reduce selfishness, and have few desires, as it is the mantra of the happiness in the life. Happiness is physical, mental and emotional state of well-being. True happiness leads to the satisfaction in the life. Happiness is, to be present, and finding the joy, in every moment of the journey of the life. Make the happiness to happen, simply by shifting the attention from the problem(s). Smile, as it creates this shift, and brings the happiness. Difficulties in the life do not come to destroy us, but to help us in realising our real strengths and true potentials. Let the difficulties of the life know, that we are much more difficult. The only way to grow is, to step out of the comfort zone, and try new things. We get confined by the walls, which we build around ourselves. Whatever a being does in his or her life, is always in the pursuit of happiness. Happiness is a characteristic of the soul. For happiness, learn to manage, the body, the mind, the emotions, and the energies. Beings are somewhat able to manage the outer, but fail miserable, when it comes to their inner management. Thoughts, mind, emotions, intellect etc. all are inner elements, which influence one's external. If the inner is being managed properly, the external will automatically get managed properly. For happiness, beings should always feel elevated in their own spaces. Stay attached for good friendship and the good relationships, which in turn, bring the happiness in life.

Change

Change is coming. Change is constant. Change is the only existing reality of this universe, and the only reality of the life. Uncertainty is the only certainty in this intriguing existence. Uncertain is certain, and the Certain is uncertain. In 1927, German Physicist Werner Heisenberg propounded the "Principle of Uncertainty", which states that, "the more precisely the position of some particle is determined, the less precisely its momentum can be predicted from initial conditions, and the vice versa". Everything is uncertain here. Birth is the death. Death is the birth. Day is the night. Night is the day. What is there today and now, will cease to exist after some time, and the new will emerge. Past goes into the space, and future emerges from the space. Space is ad infinitum. Time is ad infinitum. All the dimensions of this existence are ad infinitum. Coming and going, going and then coming, is the whole show of the life, and also, of the creation. We change at every moment. Relations and relationships also change at every moment. Situations and the circumstances associated with the life also change at every moment. Nothing is permanent here. God exists, but changes at every moment. It is the law of the creation, and is binding to all. God has made the laws, which are even binding on him as well. All and everything here, is only a change, may be big, or may be small. Birth is a change. Death is a change. In the journey of life, values are more important than the valuables. Life is a celebration. Death is shifting from one room to another room. Change is inevitable. Universe constantly changes itself, transforms itself. It is an ever-expanding universe. The cosmos is null and the infinity. Nullity and infinity both exist together. Nullity and infinity are one and the same, and the two perspectives of the same thing, created by the mind. Mind creates illusions. Except the enlightened beings, no other being can understand the life and its design, and also, of the existence. Nullity is only the Shiva. Also, Infinity is the Shiva. The coordinates of nullity and infinity are the same. Nullity is the point of origin, and also, the end for everything, here in this existence. The game and the show of the life are based on somewhere, nowhere and everywhere. Infinity is the infinite process of the change with reference to all existing dimensions, through which we all go, and are currently also going through, without an exception. This existence is the effect created out of / by the nullity and the infinity. There is no contraction, but only expansion, and it is the evolution. The universe evolves. Souls evolve. The universe always replaces, what exits our lives with another thing, which is much better and the bigger. Universe is our protector. We all are born with the approval of the universe, and all die with the approval of the universe, and then again, all are reborn with the approval of the universe. The energy of the universe is the God. Never resist the change, as change is inevitable, and is definitely for good. Do not stick to the past, and cling on or hold the things. Things and the relations of the past, lose their shine, meaning and the significance, over a definite passage of the time, and with the changing spaces, the new ones are created, which replace the older ones. There should be no void present in the life, but replaced, at the earliest. Fulfilment must be there in the life, and it comes, when the life is filled with the entities, which are needed and justly desired. Welcome the change. Change is energy. Change is a knock at the door. Welcome the change, i.e. the new energy. Let go of, what needs to be removed from the life. Weed out the weeds of the life from time to time. There are greater opportunities and blessings in surrendering and accepting. Surrendering is not the defeat, but a strategy to retain the peace of the mind, and think of something much better and bigger. Keep shining. Change brings the happiness. Change is never painful. We become rigid and stiff with the passage of time. Only the resistance to change is painful. Time creates the changes, or changes create the sense of time. Time does not wait for any being. Time does not stop for any being. The excuses in the life will not slow down the time. Indecisions in the life will not delay the time. Complaining in daily life will not stall the time. Regrets in the life will not turn back the time. Time will pass, whether utilised or unutilised. Do not waste the time in hate and anger, regrets, worries and anxieties. Do not express sorrow. Time will not turn back, and cry along with us. It is the time, which will let us go off the past, and also, make us to stop worrying about the future. Live in the present. Present is a present, i.e. a gift. The only time is now and here. Utilise this time. Explore the life. Experience the God. Experience the self. God is inside every being. Outside is essentially inside. It is the inside, which projects out. Spend the time for the right purposes with the right thoughts and the actions, filled with right emotions. Utilise the time in the company of the right beings. Time simply flies away. One can always move with the time. Spread the wings and soar with the time. We are the creator of our own life, and also, of life's destiny. Navigate the life well with the time, the best possible. The paths and the ways once crossed in the journey of the life will never come again. No one passes the same way again in the life. Keep moving; as it is the change, the desired change, good for the life. Change brings the satisfaction, and the happiness.

CHAPTER THIRTY-TWO

Mind

Make happiness a habit of the mind, an attitude, in the life. Happiness is the creation of the mind. Happiness is a certain state of the mind. Happiness cannot be learnt, but can be developed gradually with right thoughts and the actions. In the state of happiness, one sees good in everything. Feeling of happiness brings enjoyment in the life. Happy beings focus on, what they have, whereas, unhappy beings focus on, what is missing or they do not have. Do not live in the future, and also, do not remember the past, but live in the present. Believe in all the acts of the God, which are beyond control. One is always at his or her best state in the life, no matter what. Life and its design cannot be comprehended easily. Do meditation. Only enlightened beings understand the life, and also, its design. Life has not set purpose. Life is just an event like many other events of this existence. Life simply participates in the show of the creation. Life is a phenomenon among innumerable phenomena of this creation. Life is meant for experiencing. Happiness is an experience, of the soul, through the body, created by the mind. One should feel wonderful being there, where he or she is at present, and then only, it is the right state of the mind, and will bring happiness. Mind only creates happiness. Mind picks ailments, similar to the body. Therefore for a sound mind, all connections of the mind should remain, safe, secured and intact. Mind affects the body. Mind management is life management. Do Yoga. Live with the nature, in nature's style. Run, play and laugh. Eat good. Think and act good. Fulfil the needs of the journey of the life. Do not be greedy. Do not hoard and amass the things unnecessarily. All is left here only. Help others with no expectations, return or favour. Be magnanimous in behaviour and lofty in the character. Live in the exalted state. Always keep a smile on the face. Smile is the gift, given to us by the God, which can be further given to the others. Be a giver in the life, and not the taker. Giving brings pleasure, joy, satisfaction and the happiness. If all are happy, then only one can become happy. Happiness is infectious. The universe operates on a universal consciousness, which is the average of individual consciousness of all beings. Therefore, for the happiness, all beings should participate, and also contribute, in its creation and upkeep. A well-managed mind brings joy and happiness in the life. One should be mentally fit for a fit life. Mind also needs vitamins and supplements, as those, needed by the body for its proper upkeep. Mind affects us more than what our body does to us. Stresses are creations of the mind. Body bears the effects of the creations of the mind. Mind is greatly affected by the relationships. Expectations in the relationships, adversely affect, the mind, therefore, the body. Mind creates both, viz. pleasures and the pains. Give proper nutrition to the mind for its proper functioning. Mind creates the surroundings, and therefore, one's world. Mind creates all experiences of the life, some good and other bad. Program the mind to perceive the bad as good. Program the mind to remain in the state of happiness. Attachments uplift the mind. All relationships are in the mind. Good relationships lead to good mind. Keep boosting the immunity of relationships in order to keep the mind free from possible ailments like possessiveness, comparison, loneliness, misunderstandings, distrust etc.. These ailments of mind adversely affect the relationships and the life. Relationships have their direct connections and bearings with the minds. Small minds discuss beings. Medium mind discuss the events. Great minds discuss the ideas. Let the mind do not go in the isolation mode, as it may isolate the being, and make the life wretched and very unhappy. Mind needs constant careful management. Managing the mind is a great self-help. Truth is always victorious. Every being has by and large same start in his or her life, but the end is only decided by his or her karma. Purity weaves the destiny. Be heartful, and follow heartfulness. Heartfulness is a heart-centred approach towards the life, where one lives each moment of the life by the heart. Heartfulness is living naturally, in tune with the noble qualities of heart, enlightened and refined through spiritual practices. Shun arrogance, enviousness, disloyalty, anger, wrath, ego, doubt, greed, impatience and the injustice. We create our own realities in the life.

CHAPTER THIRTY-THREE

Time

Time is a non-spatial continuum, which is reckoned in terms of the events of the life, which succeed one another, from the past, through the present, running into the future. Time is a dimension. Time is needed for the existence of the being's memory. Mind memory is non-physical. Physical memory is the memory of brain of body. This physical memory dies at the time of death, but the memory of the subconscious and unconscious minds travel from one journey of the life to another. We are immortal beings. Life is infinite. The time of the journey of the life runs fast for all of us here on the earth. Time of the journey of life is finite. Earth is a low frequency vibrational plane, therefore, time moves quite fast here. In the upper spaces or planes or realms or dimensions, where vibrational frequency is very high, time moves quite slow. Spirit World is the plane or the realm or the dimension of very high vibrational frequency. Physical body cannot exist in a high vibrational plane. Only spirit body can remain in the high vibrational plane. Spirit has to don a physical garb in order to stay in a low vibrational plane like the earth. Time creates changes, or in other words, changes create the notion of the time. Success becomes the failure, or failure becomes the success, with the passage of the time. Time is not same for every being, but different for every being, as it carries different effect(s) in the life, for each one of us. What one may do in several years, other being may be able to do just in one year, or even in a lesser time. Master the energies of inside, and also, the outside, in order to win over the time. Time and space both, can be conquered by mastering the life energies, and then, the life will go the way, it is wished for. Lead a conscious life, and not a compulsive life. There are certain sciences, like Tantra, Mantra, Jaap, Meditation, Sadhna and many other techniques and methods, to communicate with the forces of the universe, and once this communication with the universe is established, things are controlled. Life can be consciously crafted. Ride the time, and control it, for creating the effects, which bring pleasure, joy and the happiness in the life. Peace is the goal of the life. Peace comes in the life, when blessings descend on the being. Universe has in its store, all kinds of things, and everything, and what is to be received; its choice is purely ours. Karma has to be done in the life. Karma means action. The kind of karma done, brings the kind of effect(s) in the life. Time affects the life, therefore, do those actions in the life, which affect the time. The two levels of the time are physical time and the spiritual time. Physical time is the motion of physical bodies. The existence of physical time depends on physical bodies. Spiritual time is desire, experience, and the spiritual motion of the soul. Spiritual time is the life of the soul. Spiritual time is the basis of the existence of the physical bodies. Beings belong to two realms viz. the phenomenal and the noumenal or the ontic. Eternity presents itself in that which is not eternal, i.e. the time processes. All time is contained in the God. Be happy in the present time. Happiness is the blessing of the God. Happiness is the feel of the God. Happiness expands the aura of the beings beyond the times and the spaces. God is beyond the time and the space.

CHAPTER THIRTY-FOUR

Space

Along with the time, space is the other very important element, which holds the entire creation, and controls the life. Space is dimensional in nature. Space is nullity, and also, the infinity. Zero and infinity are the same point on a circle (the circle of life or the existence), except the difference that zero marks the start, and infinity marks the end. Everything originates in the space (the beginning), and merges back into the space (the end). Nature of space is too difficult to comprehend, too intriguing, and also, too mysterious, like a whodunit. From where beings come, and where do they go after their death. Where fire exists? Where light exists? Where smell exists? Where air exists? All these exist in the space. Space contains everything, whether it can be sense-perceived or not. Energy exists in the space. Matter also exists in the space. We all always exist in the space, whether in the perceivable form or in the non-perceivable form. We are immortal beings. Change the space in order to bring the joy and the happiness. In nature, space is much simpler to the time. Go to a space of higher energies. Time and the space, both are the choices, which one has to make, and both of these greatly affect his or her life. Happiness is an emotion. Mood affects the emotions. Mood is created by the mind. Mind is affected by the energies. Change the energy in order to affect the mind. Live in a space of positive energies. Positive energies bring a state of well-being. Happiness is a state of well-being, which is characterised by the emotions, ranging from the contentment to the intense joy. We create our own life. Consciously exercise the freewill. Freewill is the power or the ability to make own decisions about the life rather than being controlled by any outside influence. Space inspires the beings to imagine and dream big. Anything, which can be imagined or dreamt, is a reality. Time and space are not just two words, but much more beyond that. Soul needs more space than the body, and it is the reason, why it leaves the body at the time of death. Body is a prison for the soul with limited physical space. Peace and the happiness are always right here; just one needs to create the space for these in his or her life. Sky is not the limit, as said. Curiosity is the essence of the existence. Every possibility is a reality in certain time and space coordinates. Fill the space with love. Earth is a cradle of humanity. Duality applies on space also, and thus, there is a positive space, and also, a negative space. Negative space is the space of dislike. Negative space is the space of negative energies. Stay in the positive space in order to stay happy as it contains positive energies. Also, there is a spiritual space in the process of life. The spiritual space is the sense of oneness with this creation. The spiritual space is characterised by the urge to know the purpose of existence. Spiritual space holds one's willingness to be better in everything that he or she thinks and does. A being, which progresses spiritually, no more sees him or herself, as just about an individual, but as one with the creation. Spiritual space has to do with the space, or the means, by which God could reside among his creation. Life is naturally spacious, and it's the space, which gives meaning to the life. Fill the life spaces in between. Cosmos and the spirituality overlap each other. Space is a creation of the mind. What have to be filled in the spaces of the life are always one's choice, and a result of his or her thinking and action. Fill the spaces of the life with peace, love and the happiness. It is the space, which makes various events possible like, birth, death, journey of life, astral travel, near death experiences, time travel etc. Meditation is the carrier of this experiential journey through the space. No two beings have same and similar spaces. All experiences are experienced in the space. Space and the spirituality have very close connection. Spirit or the soul needs space. Life is a mix of mass, energy, light, space and the spiritual time.

CHAPTER THIRTY-FIVE

Age

Age is just a number, an issue of the mind over the matter. Do not mind it, and then, age will not matter. Laughter is timeless and priceless. Dreams and success do not see the age, but require sincere resolution(s) to be made, which are based on planning and efforts, and you achieve, or win. Imagination sees no age. Life appreciates the age, and the nature applauds the success, when it was a challenge. Life without challenges is no life. A dead has no challenges. Challenges add colours to the life, create variation(s) in the trajectory of the life, and add to the joy and happiness. Dreams are forever. Habits die hard. If the God answers the prayers, he is increasing the faith. If the God delays in answering the prayers, he is increasing the patience. And if, the God does not answer the prayers, he has something even better. Learn that our reactions will not change anything. Beings will not start loving and respecting all of sudden. Beings minds will not change magically. It is better in the life, to let the things be, and let the beings go. Do not fight for the closure. Do not seek explanations. Do not chase the answers. Do not expect the beings to understand, where you are coming from. Learn that the life is better lived, when it is not centred on what is happening around, but centred on, what is happening inside us. Work on the self for the inner peace and the happiness. Not reacting to every little thing is the first step towards a happy and a healthy life. Do not be nincompoop. Become stone-cold sober. Do not let age become a limitation for anything. Count the age by the number of best friends. Count the life by the smiles. Age is of the body, and not of the soul or the spirit. Nothing real changes with the age. Age is a record of the life. Count the age by the experiences. Do not regret being aged, as it is a privilege denied to many, by the nature. Love and Life both have no age. Love and Life both, are limitless. Love and Life both, are beyond death. Ageing is an extraordinary process, where one becomes the kind of being, which he or she always should have been. Age is a price, paid for getting matured. Age is a price, paid for gaining the wisdom. Age is a price, paid for understanding the life. Age tells the secrets of life, the universe, the nature, and the God, and also, the secrets of the happiness. Age makes one to experience the God. Age makes one to enjoy all the relations and the relationships. Youth is a gift, but age is the work of art. With the age, pressure reduces. One needs to worry about thinking old, and not about growing old. Age is the strength. Wrinkles on the face go away with the smiles on the face. Old age is the season of harvest in the journey of life. In youth, one learns, but with the age, one understands. Old age is the time of psychological bliss. Happiness definition in the life shifts radically, but predictably, with the age. Chasing the happiness is like chasing a moving target, if it is not understood properly. Happiness is the life. To be happy, understand the life. Explore the life. Spiritual happiness happens, when the soul and the life are in sync. For many beings, age is related in a U-curve pattern to the happiness, i.e. happiness declines from youth to the middle age, but then bounces back in the old age. Religion, spirituality and/ or belief have numerous positive outcomes, especially for the older beings like enhanced health and the well-being. Religion, spirituality and / or belief help developing, much greater capacity to cope, get the social support, and the chances to participate in the society. Positive Ageing is an approach to health and well-being. Positive ageing incorporates a range of factors, which encourages an understanding of aged beings as the rounded individuals. Positive Ageing makes one to plan for, approach and live, the life's changes and challenges, with the age, in a more productive, active and fulfilling manner. Positive Ageing promotes sense of independence, dignity, well-being and the good health. Religion, spirituality and / or belief have been seen as the lenses, through which beings see and, interpret, understand, evaluate and respond to their experiences of the life. Beings who live calm and happy, do not feel the pressure of their age. Every age has its kind of happiness. Measure of happiness is looking younger than the real age. Sanity and the happiness are rare combinations. There is no path to the happiness; instead, happiness itself is the path. Nothing in the life has to be feared of, but only understood. Happiness is a choice, which one makes. Live the life, and forget the age.

CHAPTER THIRTY-SIX

Let The Existence Do Not Become Accidental

If happiness does not exist in the life, or it does not multiply, it simply means that, the very existence of that being has become purely accidental. Life should not be accidental, but consciously led. Lead the life not seriously, but sincerely. Such a being, who leads his or her life accidentally, is always a very poor manager of his or her life. Life is all about its well-management, and he or she is unable to manage the life, the way, it should have been. Manage the mind. Mind is villain, if not managed. Mind becomes hero, if well-managed. Mind is a tool, and not the master. For every being, the techniques to manage the life may be same, but the rigour of their implementation is very different, and not same, which makes their life different. Mostly, beings remain sad, and a very few beings only remain happy. Happiness is the treasure of the life. Happy beings are living their life in blessings, whereas, unhappy or sad beings are living their life under bane or curse. Blessings or bane are being's creations. Yoga and Meditation are simple life management techniques. Being grateful and thankful is a practice of life management. Prayer is also a simple life management technique. Prayers, if done sincerely, greatly impact the mind. Learn to efficiently manage the body, mind, emotions and the energies, as doing so, only manages the life. All external experiences are actually, created and felt inside. Inside is only the outside. Outside may affect the inside, only if, inside or the inner, is poorly managed. Practise the Inner Engineering. Inner Engineering is the process of creating a balance between the challenges of day-to-day life and the inner longing for well-being and peace, and this all is very easily achievable by Yoga and Meditation practices. Holistically, Yoga means connecting the self with the God, and it happens by doing Yoga. Understand the engineering of the life, i.e. Life Engineering. Heaven and the Hell, are inner creations i.e. mind's creations, and manifested outwardly. Life is all about the peace of the mind, and the peace of the mind is all about, to never mind. If mind is at peace, journey of the life becomes a celebration. Life is a journey of infinite miles. A good journey happens, only by the right steps, which are taken for it. Inner management is very crucial for a meaningful life. Every being's creation is with certain purpose(s), definite purpose(s), and let the purpose(s) be fulfilled by exercising, the real and true potential, which the God has already given with the birth, to each one of us. Anxiety develops, when the existence becomes accidental. Bad management of the life develops stress(s) in the life. Thinking and the thought are inner, whereas, actions are largely external. Outside can never be managed, as it is simply the outcome of the various inner processes, i.e. mind's activities. One should have control of his or her own systems; otherwise everything becomes too uncontrolled and stressful. One's works are never stressful, but the ways of executing these works, which are inner driven, may make these works stressful. Other's minds can only be managed, when the self-mind is well-managed. Beings should rise to their full potential in terms of peace, love and the compassion, as it is very important for their well-being, other's well-being, and eventually bringing the happiness to them, and to the others, and to this vast creation. Earn the success based on the service to others, and not at the expense of others. Doing good for others, is not only our duty, but also, it is one of the biggest joy of the life, and it improves the health, and brings immense happiness in the life. Also, it is an order of the God for each one of us. If you want to be heard, never sing in chorus. Happiness is our creation.

CHAPTER THIRTY-SEVEN

I Am The Divine Flame

We are divine. We are eternal. We never die. Our essence never dies. We are immortals. The real me always exists. It has to exist for this existence to exist. No physical death of any kind is an accident or untimely and unwanted. Every death of every sort is strictly as per the divine plan, the great design of the creation. Everything happens at its right time. Love, faith, attitude and positive thinking help handle the toughest times of the life with ease and calm. Never compare your life with the life of others. Sun and the moon cannot be compared for they shine at different moments, i.e. in their times, and they have different purposes. We glow differently, when we have good beings with good intentions in the life. Life is never easy for any being. Life had been too difficult for the gods and the incarnations of the God. Life has to be made easy by ignoring and accepting the things. Be the lion, and all will be ours, just ours. This existence is for us, by us and because of us. And, what we are, is because of the self, others, surroundings, environment and the nature. It's a fallacy to believe that money brings happiness. Peace and the happiness are internal, and never external. Attain the divinity. Creator and the creation are never different. Creator is inside the creation, similar to, as every pottery carries the reflection, impressions, signature, thought and actions of its maker. Soul is the element of the God inside each one of us. Soul is being's essence, and the real identity. Thus, already there is the divinity within each one of us. Life itself is divinity. As long as divine flame glows inside the physical body, one is in the body and the body is alive. Physical body needs power and the energy of the universe, for it to exist and work. These are called life forces. Integration of life forces with the physical body is the birth, and detachment is the death. Force is created by the energy. The energy is being's consciousness. Energy is the God. Consciousness is soul. Soul is an ever glowing flame, i.e. the divine flame. Birth occurs, when the divine flame starts glowing. Love is the divine flame. Beings efforts should be to give wings to the divine flame and fill the whole creation and the existence with its glow of goodness. We are reflection of one another. Twin flames always meet. A Twin Flame is an intense soul connection with someone thought to be a being's other half. It is also called as the "Mirror Soul." Sometimes soul gets split into two bodies. Passion is the fire. We all are here on the Physical Plane i.e. earth, for following our passions. Interestingly, the brightest flame casts darkest shadow. One is never alone, never empty. The God kindles this divine flame. Life is a pure flame. Acknowledging the goodness is the foundation of abundance and happiness in the life. Do the things that make you happy. Boost mental and physical energy levels. Do the Divine Flame Meditation. The three stages in meditation are, to feel, to hear, and to see. Spiritual life aims at realisation of unity. In meditation, we rise above the tendency of separatism and enter into unity. Meditation is renouncing the fragments. Meditation is entering into the communion with the whole. To meditate is to navigate. With Violet Flame Meditation, one can consciously access the powerful fifth dimensional frequencies. Violet Flame Meditation dissolves lifetimes of unresolved and unhealed energies with the love and the light. The distillation of all experiences beings ever had in any lifetime or dimension is still in their individual and group energy fields, which can be positive or negative. The dense negativity must be transmuted into the love and the light, in order to annihilate the resulting chaos, which all have unfortunately experienced for eons.

CHAPTER THIRTY-EIGHT

The Farewell

Bid adieu to all, and to everything, and go, and rest in peace. Go peacefully and happily in the lap of the God. God is greatest, joy, happiness, love and peace. There is no danger but full protection, full safety and full security. Death must be dignified. Death is "right" turn, at a right time, and at the right place, during the journey of the life, on the physical plane i.e. the earth. Death is a great farewell. A great farewell aims at bringing more happiness than the before, in the onward journey in future. Death is an end, as well as, a beginning. If there is no death, there will be no birth either. As we welcome birth, in the similar manner, we should also welcome death. Birth is an act of the nature; death is also an act of the nature. Nature never does anything wrong. The show of creation has to go on, and yet, changes have to occur continuously, therefore, there is no other way except the grand farewell, i.e. the death, after the birth. Death must occur in the state of happiness. The state of death decides the next course of life. It is a secret. During the death, being must be at utter peace and calm, and if possible, in the state of happiness. Death is a reunion with all those loved ones, who have died before. In this creation, there is unification and separation. Souls always live in groups, whether here in the Physical

World during the journey of the life, of there in the Spirit World, after the death. There are soul families in the Spirit World. Live a great life. Do not aspire for a long life. Life should be big. Death is decided at the time of the birth, or even before the birth, by the soul or the spirit, going to carnate itself. We decide our own life. We are in this existence always. We are immortals. Our real identity is the soul inside. Soul is consciousness. Soul is energy. Energy can neither be created nor destroyed. Energy can be transformed. We are in this journey of life because we had died in the previous journey. We all have taken birth and died innumerable times before, in the past, and the same will occur again in the future, up to the time infinity. It is how the God has designed this existence. Except the God, there is duality for everything. For Birth, it is death. And for death, it is birth. For day, it is night. For white, it is black. For positive, it is negative. Negative energy is needed for the positive energy to exist. The existence of positive energy is only because the negative energy exists. Due to resistance, there is current flow in an electric circuit. If there is no resistance, there will be no current. Due to friction only, we are able to walk. If there is no friction, we cannot walk. If there are no pains, there will be no pleasures. Success is due to failure. Interestingly, the thing which opposes something, is also the very cause of that thing, to occur or to happen or to exist. Since there are takers, there are givers. Thus, the balance or equilibrium is created and maintained. Good exists because bad exists. If there is no bad, there will be no good either. Since, there is a "happy welcome", there is "the farewell", which should also be happy, i.e. "the happy farewell". Happiness is the life. Life is a drama. We are its scriptwriter. Write a happy script for life. Do not fret or cry for it is over, but smile and be happy, for it happened. Try to see the glass half full. Create a right attitude in the life. Life is a celebration. There is not even a single reason to get sad or unhappy in the life. Manage the mind. See the things in the right perspective. Have positive thinking. Lead a conscious life. What is being chosen, shapes the life. Use the power of subconscious mind. It is never a goodbye, but it is always, a see you later. Every new dawn, opens up a new chapter of the book of life. Be brave enough to say goodbye, so that life reward with a new hello. Art of beginning is great, but the art of ending is greater. Our roads are different, our journeys are different, but our destination is same. Our source is also same. We are one and the same, just a reflection of one another. No one ever dies. There is no farewell, but always a thank you, and expression of gratitude. Death is the nature's way of telling to slow down, take a turn, and then move on, in the right direction. Death is for another life, a new family, new friends, new things, new experiences; new script of the life, with few or more, previous life journey's loved ones, once again together here also, in the new roles. Death is a change of the costumes. Death is just change of the room. All gets renewed after the death, i.e. the farewell. The farewell provides opportunities for healing and rejuvenation. The farewell – and I shall see your happy face some day again in the clouds...

CHAPTER THIRTY-NINE

Refuel Your Soul

Refuel yourself. Refuel your soul each day. Good thoughts and good actions refuel the soul. Speak truth; be honest, compassionate and selfless. It goes without saying that beings should exhibit divine qualities and best of the human traits. Live a well-lived life. A normal being dies many times in a lifetime. Whenever, something is thought and done against the conscience, soul is wounded, and the being dies. Listen to the voice of the soul. Soul is the pure energy, free from any impurity, an element of the God, in each one of us. After the death, spirit is being healed up and refuelled in the Spirit World. In the Physical World, spirit gets weak and weaker. There are many hurts, wounds and scars on the soul, which get created, during the journey of the life in the Physical World, i.e. on the earth. During sleep, spirit or soul is healed and rejuvenated. God's love refuels the soul. Love refuels the soul. Hatred, enviousness, anger, anxiety and worry, simply sap out or weaken the soul or the spirit. Take pause. Adversities are needed in the life, as brakes are needed in the vehicle. A brake opposes the movement, but gives the confidence to take the vehicle for a journey. Also, brakes provide the needed controls for the vehicle during the journey. Similarly, challenges, trying situations and circumstances, bad events and failures are needed for a successful and meaningful life. Do not be a self-consumed being. Help all those, who are in their dire straits. Be a giver. Be a healer. Be the source of positive energy. Exude charm. Send good vibes. Be grateful for the blessings in the life. Life is never a straight path for any being. Take deep breath and relax. Do Yoga and Meditation. Maintain sanity. Give the soul a chance to catch up with the body. Enjoy with family and the friends. Change something daily, in order to change the life. The secret of success and the happiness is found in the daily routine. Starve the ego. Do not ever give up. For any recharge, renewal is very necessary. Nowhere, a being can find a quieter or more untroubled retreat than in his or her soul. Give all your worries, troubles and pains to the God. Ask the heaven, where my child or the loved one is, as heaven knows about it, and everything. Keep love in the heart and the peace in the mind, in order to bring joy and happiness in the life. Whatever is demanded by the soul, do that, and the soul will get refuelled. Hydrate the soul in the stream of love and care of the nature, in the nature's ways. As the glass mirror shows the face, in a similar manner, works of art, show the soul, therefore, be creative, work on the passions and the hobbies.

CHAPTER FORTY

Hard Work

Hard work is the key to happiness. Learn from failures. Have belief in the self, and self-capabilities. Hard work leads to the success. Success is no accident, but a result of the hard work only. Success brings joy and happiness in the life. Love, what is being done? Stay positive. Hard work beats the talent. Without hard work nothing prospers. In the journey of life, happiness in itself is a journey, and not any destination. Think of the destination as the purpose, and think of the journey as the things to be done, which make one happy. We do not get, what is wished for, instead we get, what we work for. Hard work has no substitute. Success has no shortcuts. Never discourage a being, which continually makes the progress, no matter how slow. Work is worship. Live united, united with everything, in this God's creation. Everything is me only, just another me. United we stand. Be thankful to everything, especially to the godsend. Godsend is something unexpected, which is very useful, as it has come just, when it is needed. The existence belongs more to those beings, which are energetic and hard working. Work hard in silence, and let, success roar. The chance and the ability to the hard work, in itself, is an opportunity, which is denied to many. Opportunities come, disguised as the hard work, recognise it, work hard on it. Hard work is the purpose of life, therefore, give whole heart and soul to it. Hard work overcomes hard luck. Imagine, believe and achieve, it is the secret of success and all other achievements in the life. Never give up. With the hard work, greatness befalls automatically. Beings rise to fame and glory by the dint of sheer hard work. There are no shortcuts in the life. Be patient. Be disciplined. Do not procrastinate the things, do it today, and now, tomorrow never comes. Learn the value and importance of the hard work by working hard. Some beings want it to happen, other wish it would happen, but a few ones, make it to happen. Cherish the good moments and the experiences of the life. Stay focussed at your goals. Choices made in the life, show what we truly are. Talent without hard work is a tragedy. Keep yourself engaged positively. In the absence of positive, negative will take its place. Mind has a tendency to either indulge in the positive, or in the negative, but it cannot remain neutral. Work on the mind. Do Yoga and the Meditation. Do prayers. Keep the mind at peace. Connect the self, with the nature, the universe and the God. Be thankful to all those beings, who have come in your life, be it father, or mother, or brother, or sister, or wife, or son, or daughter, or colleague, or friend, or relative, or neighbour, or any other being. It is all, as per the grand design. Every single thing makes the journey of life possible, whether in the perception or not. Best is, thank every single thing, in this creation. Opportunities are given by the God. What is done with the talent and the opportunities, which comes one's way, is being's freewill and the choice. Freewill is the power or the ability to make the decisions in the life, rather than being force-guided or controlled by any outside influence. Is freewill, really free? Do self-discovery. Identify your gift, which the God has gifted to you, and then, work hard to build it. Be patient. Have faith and belief. Results of hard work will come, may be a little late, it is God's design. For every cause, there is always an effect. Hard work is the cause, and its effect is its result. Every being has his or her design of the life; therefore, never compare self with the others. You are "the best", as you are. Work on the weaknesses to convert these into strengths. Interestingly, weakness is the strength, and strength the weakness, all is how, situations are being perceived and responded to. Think good, and act good, goodness and the happiness will simply follow, it is the law, the law of nature, the law of universe, and God's order. All are born rich, and not poor, identify the richness, which you have. Richness lies in the thoughts. All are born happy, and not sad, identify the happiness, and try retaining it. Happiness lies in the thoughts. Life is beautiful. God is great. Shower the love, which you have, on everything, and the God will shower his love and grace on you. Grace is what the God does, as he is all gracious. Every action of the God toward us involves his grace. Be thankful to the God for his providence. Always look at the bigger picture, and you will always remain happy.

CHAPTER FORTY-ONE

Learn To Live Alone

We all are alone. Learn to live alone. Not everyone will stay beyond a time, or forever. Living alone develops inner strength. Living alone is an opportunity. We have come on this planet all alone at the time of the birth. Also, we die alone. End of every being is in the loneliness. Parents, siblings and others are only co-travellers or companions for some part or the portion of the journey of life. Always, we only save ourselves. We ourselves have to walk all the paths and undertake all the journeys. Being alone is a power. Sun is alone, but shines. Avoid company of those beings, which do not value you. One of the greater gifts, which can be given to someone, is the time. Time given, is that portion of the time of the life of being, which will never return to him or her. Learn the importance of time. Invest the time, and do not squander it. No single being, which started with you, will also, finish with you. As a matter of fact, no other being started with us in the physical life. Time and space coordinates of physical life, including birth and death, for every being are simply unique, and no two beings have the same coordinates. One of the hard lessons of the life is, how to be alone all over again, while still being happy. Do not create any undue attachment with any being and anything in the life, as it will, sooner or later, become source of great distress, deep sorrow and excruciating pain(s). Why to writhe in the pain, if proper understanding can be developed, and such a situation can be easily avoided or circumvented. Give everything, every relation and relationship, its real meaning. Respect all, and unconditionally love all. Do not expect any favour or return. There should be no expectations and comparisons in the life. Better to learn, to forget, and to forgive. What is wished for in the life, will never come easy in the life. Our mind also gives more importance and value to that which is not easily accessible or achievable. Do not be afraid of walking alone, as it is the fact of the life. Being alone has many apparent benefits, as no one cheats on you, hurts you, and threatens you, and many more others. In loneliness, we restore ourselves, we rejuvenate ourselves. If you want to be heard, never sing in chorus. In loneliness also, one is in the company of loneliness itself, and many others, which are always present and accompanying us in this vast, mysterious and enigmatic existence, may be in the physical form, or may be in the spirit form i.e. the non-physical. There is always a certain sound of the silence. There is always a certain light in the darkness. There is always a certain peace and pleasure and the happiness, in the chaos, confusion and the commotion. Life is all about, how the mind takes it. God is always accompanying us. Sorrow and happiness are the creations of the mind. Train the mind. Manage the mind. Mind is the not the master, but the slave. Many times, we have to stand alone, just to ensure, that "I can". We need a break, many times in the life, to explore, to figure out something. Being alone is not becoming unhappy, but to become happier than before. In loneliness, one is always in the company of his or her real self or the true self. Enlightenment happens in the loneliness, and not in the midst of the maddening crowd, or in a company. It is equally better to live alone, and walk alone, instead of going in the wrong direction. Being alone, is also, a design of the life, approved by the God. Some beings come into the life, only to teach, how to live alone, and / or to tell us experientially, to start living alone from now on. Love solitude and the silence. Silence is not the death, but a birth. Every end is a new beginning. When a seed rips open to sprout through the soil, or the chick breaks open the egg shell, it is utter silence and the loneliness. Energy integrates and conserves, only in the silence and the loneliness, otherwise the energy simple dissipates and gets wasted. Equilibrium is reached, only when, all the disturbances are over. Travelling alone is one of the most liberating experiences of the life. All right answers are found, when being alone. It takes courage to stand alone. Love, relations and the presence of being(s), are valued in the loneliness. Loneliness provides an opportunity of self-discovery. Meaningful silence is always better than meaningless words. Many a times, sad souls hide behind the happy faces. Strong being is strongest, when alone. Happy being is happiest, when alone. When alone talk to the universe, talk to the God, play with the nature. In, the journey of the life, the journey of success and prosperity, or the spiritual journey, one is always alone. It is better to walk alone, than with the fool(s). Being together is not always good. We become, and we are, what we do. Every being is an individuated consciousness of the universe, which is not further divisible. Something, which cannot be further divided, is always alone. At the end of a long division process, only cipher or zero is left, which cannot be further divided. Cipher or zero means emptiness or nothingness. It is the state of complete dissolution, i.e. integration with the

God, and then happiness simply turns into the bliss.

CHAPTER FORTY-TWO

Be Creative

Creation is the biggest act. It is an art. Be creative. Contribute in this vast existence through creations. Only, energy can create the energy. Only, life can create the life. Creation is the life. A dead cannot create anything. Matter with the help of energy can create other matter. Energy is the impelling or main driving force behind this creation, and its everything. Creativity is the power to connect the seemingly unconnected. Creativity brings inner joy, peace and the happiness. Creation is difficult. Destruction is easy. Creation creates positive energy, and brings happiness in the life. Creation happens because of the positive energy. Destruction happens because of the negative energy. Creativity is the ability to make or to produce new things, by using skill or the imagination. Creativity is knowledge, more it is used, more gets produced and accumulated. Creativity is sheer intelligence. Creativity brings innovation. Soul is creative, and this creativity of the soul makes the life beautiful. Creativity entails freedom, a free mindset i.e. a mind, which is not set. Mindset is general attitude of a being. Mindset means fixed ideas i.e. the set mind, which is often too difficult to change. Creativity fills itself in the empty spaces of the mind, if allowed. Creativity has no limits. Ideas can come from anything and everything. A creative being possesses all the courage to let go of the certainties. In this show of the life, only uncertain is certain. Creativity is too contagious, spread it. Inspiration comes from a being, which is creative, and also working. Do not wait for inspiration, as it simply comes while working. Creativity allows mistakes. Mistakes are teachers of the life. Every being should start from where he or she is, use whatever he or she has, and do whatever he or she can, as it is only, "being creative". Do not doubt self-abilities. Doubt is the biggest enemy of creativity. Doubt is a negative force, deterring and intimidating in its nature. Involve fun, while being creative, doing something creatively. This creation is the canvas of God's creativity mixed with his imagination. Every imagination is a reality. A wildest imagination is a distant reality, which can be very easily achieved in the remote future. Even the mirage is a reality, as to perceive something, it has to exist. For false to exist, false has to be true. This universe is the game of duality. A thing and its exact opposite co-exist, meaning existing in the same time and space coordinates. Dream is a reality. Which cannot be sense-perceived, but there is a thought about it, is also a reality, and can be very easily created. Mind has the power to do anything and everything. We ourselves are the universe. We are full creation. Inside is only outside. We are the gods. Rise in love with yourself first. Work hard, come out of comfort zones. Solitude and silence promote the creativity. Solitude refreshes the soul. Balanced activities, yoga, rest, sleep and meditation kindle creativity. Creativity is, piercing the mundane. Make creativity a habit, and do something creative each day in the journey of the life. Creativity is finding the marvellous. Be artistic. Think out of the box, as it is only called creative thinking. Give yourself, permission to become creative. Creativity is the science behind the madness, leading to the excellence. Think smart. Standout, do lots of work and do not be lazy, be curious, take pause between the work, take a nap when necessitated, take rest, eat good food and juicy fruits, drink lots of water as hydration is very necessary, absorb rare and diverse influences, travel a lot, greet and meet beings, go for long walks, jog, relax, pray, talk to the nature, live with the nature nature's style, stop overthinking, give all troubles and problems of the life to the God, be thankful, express gratitude, lead a simple life and help the others; these are simple steps to "be creative", and then, to become happy through its manifestation. Good thoughts and good actions are the bases for every single good thing in the life.

CHAPTER FORTY-THREE

The Secret Of Happiness

There is no other bigger mystery and the secret, than the life. Life is the biggest mystery and the secret, and so are its all associated things. What happens, why it happened, when it will happen, why we are here, what is the purpose of the life, are just few of many baffling queries and questions of the life. Only the enlightened beings know about it. Take the life sincerely, and not seriously. Watch the life, as a spectator, a witness, instead getting involved it, entangled into it. Life is meant for experiencing, with no reactions in any case, but few responses in few cases. Experience the every taste of life. We all come again and again in a new journey of the life for getting new and newer experiences of the life. Ignore and try forgetting bad things, bad beings and their behaviour. Forgive such beings, as they are also your reflection. Never judge others. Nothing remains same here, and changes the very next moment. Good may turn into bad, and bad into good. Live like a king, a king-size life. Think big. Keep lofty aims, goals and objectives in the life. Dedicate everything to the God; let it be success or failure, happiness or sorrow, or birth or death. Without God's will and nature's approval, no big event is possible in the life. In the life, certain things are just beyond control, then why to bother about them. We are just a speck of dust here in this infinite existence. We do not run this existence. Even we do not run our lives. We are just an insignificant player here in the game of the life, and an insignificant actor in the show of the life. This landscape belongs to every species here, equally and equitably. Do not push your claims on anything. Nothing is yours. Responsibility comes along with accountability. Equity and equality always go together. There is nothing superior or inferior here in this creation. These are wrong notions, and false creations of the mind. All are "the best" in their designs. Shed the ego. There is nothing like "I", but there is a definite "We". Life is a continuous journey. Karma is carry forwarded from one journey of the life to another. We are makers of our own life trajectories. We are the architects of our own lives. Manifest plainness, embrace simplicity, reduce selfishness, and have few desires, as it is the mantra of the happiness in the life. Listen with curiosity, speak with honesty, and act with integrity. Everything in the life happens just at its right time. Give time to the time. Death does not occur before the death. There are certain designed time and space coordinates for everything of the life. The secret of happiness is the freedom, and the secret of freedom is the courage. Be courageous. Always be grateful in the life for everything, which is there in the life. In the life, every sunrise must hold the promises, and every sunset must hold the peace. Express your gratitude, and also, be thankfulness to the others, and to every other thing, which is the part of the life. One's life is supported by innumerable visible and invisible things and objects, energies, spirits and the beings. Keep smiling, and do not hurt other(s). These are the simple ways, leading towards the happiness in the life, i.e. the secrets of happiness. Happiness is a journey, and not any destination. Love yourself. Love the God. God is inside us. Discover your qualities and the abilities, as it helps in the appreciation of the self. Similarly, discover the qualities and abilities of other beings, in order to appreciate them equally, or if possible, more than the self. Me, my and myself should come at the last. Discovery of qualities and the abilities, gives rise to the love, love with the self, and love for the others. Make nature your friend. Talk to birds, animals, trees, river and mountains. Interact with love with everything in this creation. Discovery of qualities and abilities creates the importance of self, and also, of the others, in the life. Discovery of the qualities and abilities in the other being(s), creates a cooperative and harmonious relationship, and companionship, and eventually, brings pleasure, joy, peace, satisfaction and the happiness, in the life. Closeness or the nearness, and the love for the God, are based on the discovery of attributes related to the God. Be modest and humble. Pay your respect to the forces of the nature. The attributes of the God are powers, mercy and the compassion, which are very easily evident in the surroundings. God definitely exists. There is definitely a supreme energy, running the show of the life, and this entire creation. This creation is a play of matter and energy. Matter is ephemeral, but the energy is eternal. The God being creator of everything is the aspect, which builds the strongest relationship of love with the God. The God created everything from nothing. Infinity originated from nullity. Nullity and the infinity are the same points facing in the opposite directions. Sorrow is the happiness, facing in the opposite direction. Through actions, try changing its direction. It is the secret of bringing happiness in the life. God is the reason for everything, and of the existence of all. We have been fashioned into this existence by the God. God creates our worlds to live. The world has been created to be favourable and propitious. Everything in the existence is such that it helps us to unfold our real potential, and then, allows us to grow to any extent. In every failure, there is a great learning, and many other hidden positive aspects. Everything in the life is the design created by the God. Success is not our achievement, and not created by us, but there is a direct hand of the God in it. Submit yourself completely before the God, in order to become happy in the life. Prostrate or bow down before the God. Discovery of the creator leads to the discovery of humility within, or to say, that the humility leads to the discovery of the God, and the discovery of peace, satisfaction and the happiness. Happiness is the goal and the very purpose of the life. Physical possessions, wealth, worldly relations and attachments can never bring the happiness in the life, but one's religious and spiritual accomplishments bring the satisfaction and the happiness. Live the life with full understanding. Spirituality is quite essential in the life, in order to explore the life, love the life, and live the life meaningfully. Happiness is never external, but purely internal. Overthinking steals the happiness. Do not create the walls, but live in openness, i.e. in the state of complete freedom. God has provided every single thing in the life to enjoy and to share, and not for amassing and storage. More conclusions we make, less alive we become. If something is doable, then do it with full involvement. It would be very remiss of beings, if they do not perform their duties sincerely with complete awakening, and in the state of full consciousness. When you walk this planet, sense all that, which is amiss, and correct it with best of your efforts.

Every right endeavour is being rewarded. The existence also runs on the premise of "Reward and Punishment". A happy being is happy, not because everything is just right in his or her life, but he or she is happy because his or her attitude towards everything in his or her life is just right. All happiness is inside only. Outside is essentially inside. Carry no expectations in order to be happy, and to remain happy. Always, demonstrate an attitude of gratitude. Be thankful, in order to become happy. Right perspective in the life is necessary to remain happy in the life, as happiness is a perspective. The life goes on, in its own ways and styles. See the glass half full, and not the empty. Do not hold the things and keep the attachments. Shower unconditional love. Live with, full detachments in the attachments, in order to be happy in the life. Happiness is the craziest equation of the mathematics of the life, as it multiplies, when being divided, and it corrects the physics and chemistry of the life. There is a Law of Attraction. Think of the happiness, invite the happiness in the life, and the happiness will simply come in the life. Expect the unexpected. Believe the impossible. Life unfolds itself in numerous ways, simply beyond the guesses and comprehension.

CHAPTER FORTY-FOUR

Amazing Life Secrets

Challenges make the life interesting, and overcoming these challenges, make the life meaningful. Do not live the same day again. Umbrella cannot stop the rain, but makes us to stand in the rain, and face it, similarly, confidence may not bring the success, but gives the power to stand and face the problems and tough and tougher situations of the life. Give your hands to serve, and your hearts to love. Happiness in the life comes by having the purpose and the sense of meaning of the life. An intelligent being opens the mind, a beautiful being opens the eyes, and a loving being opens the heart. Do not torture, torment, punish and burden yourself with excessive regret for the past. Let bygones be bygones. Do not cling to a bad past, as beautiful future eagerly awaits us. We all make mistakes. Do not be too harsh to yourself for the committed mistakes. Past cannot be undone. Learn from the past, and do not repeat the same mistakes in the present or in the future. Do not believe anything, which goes against the commonsense, unless you have the first hand proof. If you are not applying, what you already know, and then there is no point of being so intent on gaining what you do not know. Always, use the reason(s) and the discretion before accepting or trusting something or someone. Let the consciousness work fully. Life gives us more, only when, we rightly use, what we already have. Knowledge changes the life. The life, never throws the challenge(s), which a being just cannot handle. Challenges are put forth to every being depending upon his or her ability and capacity to handle these and bear; such is the amazing design of the life. Life is never too burdening for any being. Always be positive, and also, be grateful to everything. We are not just we, but we are everything. Very little is needed to make a life happy, as it is all within the self, i.e. in the ways of thinking. Thought becomes the action. Never measure the life by the possessions, instead, measure the life by the number of hearts touched, the smiles created, and the love showered and shared. Shift the attention from problems to the blessings, for happiness in the life. Create your identity in such a way that beings start realising their loss, when ignoring or leaving you. Live with grace, dignity and the uniqueness. Live with greatness. Be honest, and do fair dealings. Things have to end for better things to begin. Take genuine interest in daily life details. Do not think about, what others will think about you. This is your life, and only you are its maker. Discover the life. Life is easy and good. Talk to the universe, as you talk to your family members, and friends. Universe responds, and also, acts on requests. Sometimes be alone, and if you want to cry, cry. Tears should not be kept in. Enjoy the passage of time, and the given journey of the life. Like, what is being done by you. Accept your position and the situations. Acceptance brings peace to the mind. Try to make the most out of every day. There is no situation, which beings cannot change. Thoughts are cause of everything. Work on hobbies and passions, as doing so, is working meditation, and the powers of the universe and the God can be experienced that time. The energy of the universe works though us. We always stay tuned to the universe, therefore, for descend of better and positive energies of the universe within you, raise your level of vibrations. God is a frequency, a definite vibration. In the state of melancholy or the depression, bad and negatives energies influence us. Make self-aura strong and stronger, as it provides a strong safety jacket to protect us from the harm created by the negative influences, negative powers and the negative energies. We all have been brought in this universe with certain purpose(s). Nothing and no being are redundant here, as such a redundant thing or the being can simply not exist. Causality is in the root of everything. For every effect, there is a definite cause. Do fret or worry about the effects, but look into and analyse the cause(s). Correct the cause(s) in order to get the desired effect(s). Work in harmony with the nature, and never ever go against it. God is everywhere. Do not become selfish. Help others. Listen to the soul, and act, accordingly. Gold is found in the dirt. Do not pooh-pooh the things, and treat the beings with contempt, as it is not only totally uncalled for, but also, an act of displeasing and dishonouring the God. We are here in the Physical World for limited time, therefore, life peacefully, in full love and complete harmony, and happily. Share the things. No being has ever become poor by giving. God gives more to us, for sharing, and giving those things to the needy. Life should have some purpose. Do not get trapped in the trap of karma. Karma creates an inexorable vicious cycle. Life is not happening to us, but we create it, for us. Forget and forgive for happiness in the life. Who are there in the life, is more important than, what is there in the life. Live in the present moment, as if, there is no next or future moment. Never quit. Stay young. This existence is a strange play of duality. Accept the both, the good side, and also, the bad side. Positive energy exists due to the existence of the negative energy. Swords and words have the same letters. Do not condemn and contemn yourself, and also, the others. Constancy of the purpose is the secret of the success. Every being has to learn the secrets of life by himself. Learn to let go. Be kind in the nature, and demonstrate the kindness through the actions. Mind is everything, therefore, work on the mind, and manage the mind. Do yoga and meditation. Love is the necessary element in everything done or acted upon, as it brings satisfaction, pleasure, joy, peace and the happiness.